Cambridge Elements

Elements in the Philosophy of Physics
edited by
James Owen Weatherall
University of California, Irvine

PHILOSOPHY OF COSMOLOGY AND ASTROPHYSICS

Siska De Baerdemaeker
Stockholm University

Shaftesbury Road, Cambridge CB2 8EA, United Kingdom

One Liberty Plaza, 20th Floor, New York, NY 10006, USA

477 Williamstown Road, Port Melbourne, VIC 3207, Australia

314–321, 3rd Floor, Plot 3, Splendor Forum, Jasola District Centre, New Delhi – 110025, India

103 Penang Road, #05–06/07, Visioncrest Commercial, Singapore 238467

Cambridge University Press is part of Cambridge University Press & Assessment, a department of the University of Cambridge.

We share the University's mission to contribute to society through the pursuit of education, learning and research at the highest international levels of excellence.

www.cambridge.org
Information on this title: www.cambridge.org/9781009538862

DOI: 10.1017/9781009227995

© Siska De Baerdemaeker 2025

This publication is in copyright. Subject to statutory exception and to the provisions of relevant collective licensing agreements, no reproduction of any part may take place without the written permission of Cambridge University Press & Assessment.

When citing this work, please include a reference to the DOI 10.1017/9781009227995

First published 2025

A catalogue record for this publication is available from the British Library

ISBN 978-1-009-53886-2 Hardback
ISBN 978-1-009-22795-7 Paperback
ISSN 2632-413X (online)
ISSN 2632-4121 (print)

Cambridge University Press & Assessment has no responsibility for the persistence or accuracy of URLs for external or third-party internet websites referred to in this publication and does not guarantee that any content on such websites is, or will remain, accurate or appropriate.

For EU product safety concerns, contact us at Calle de José Abascal, 56, 1°, 28003 Madrid, Spain, or email eugpsr@cambridge.org

Philosophy of Cosmology and Astrophysics

Elements in the Philosophy of Physics

DOI: 10.1017/9781009227995
First published online: August 2025

Siska De Baerdemaeker
Stockholm University

Author for correspondence: Siska De Baerdemaeker,
siska.debaerdemaeker@philosophy.su.se

Abstract: Cosmology and astrophysics provide a unique resource for philosophers of science: due to novel physics, the remoteness of their targets, and the range of relevant spatiotemporal scales, research in these areas pushes the methodology of empirical science to its limits. It should therefore not be surprising that philosophy of cosmology, and, to a lesser degree, philosophy of astrophysics, have seen an explosive growth over the past two decades. This Cambridge Element surveys the existing literature, identifies areas for future research, and highlights how philosophy of cosmology and astrophysics have implications for debates in general philosophy of science.

Keywords: philosophy of cosmology and astrophysics, cosmic inflation, dark matter, dark energy, black holes

© Siska De Baerdemaeker 2025

ISBNs: 9781009538862 (HB), 9781009227957 (PB), 9781009227995 (OC)
ISSNs: 2632-413X (online), 2632-4121 (print)

Contents

1 Introduction   1
2 Cosmic Inflation   6
3 Dark Matter   19
4 Dark Energy   30
5 Black Holes   39
6 Empiricism, Epistemology, and Ethics   49
7 Conclusion   64

    References   66

1 Introduction

Cosmology and astrophysics push scientific methodology to its limits. Their worldly targets are remote, covering spatiotemporal scales beyond the reach of any practically conceivable terrestrial experiment. Some of their targets are unique. They study regimes where our current best physical theories are expected to break down. And several types of novel physics have been introduced purely on cosmological or astrophysical grounds. At face value, this seems reason enough to be skeptical of their epistemic success: how can science ever succeed in such dire circumstances?

Yet current consensus is that cosmology and astrophysics have been quite successful in reconstructing the evolution of our universe and of astrophysical objects. For one, several Nobel Prizes in Physics from the past two decades have rewarded research in cosmology and astrophysics, ranging from the study of black holes, gravitational waves, and exoplanets, to the accelerated expansion of the universe and the Cosmic Microwave Background radiation. My first goal in this Element is to explore the many ways cosmology and astrophysics have been successful, despite the challenges these disciplines face. I will show that the methodology of cosmology and astrophysics is extremely rich. Any broad-brush claims about "lack of empirical access" are therefore unwarranted, even though there are certainly contexts where the available empirical resources are limited.

The success of cosmology and astrophysics also implies an unusual opportunity for philosophers of science. These disciplines can provide a testing bed for various philosophical views on the epistemology and metaphysics of science. Do they hold up when applied to cosmological and astrophysical research? My second goal is therefore to highlight by demonstration how much philosophy of science stands to gain from paying close attention to cosmology and astrophysics. Along the way, it will become clear that the reverse is also true: philosophy of science can provide useful resources for resolving existing controversies in cosmology and astrophysics.

This Element introduces the rich body of philosophical scholarship on cosmology and astrophysics that has emerged in recent years, and it points to areas ripe for philosophical investigation. It does not purport to give an exhaustive overview of all topics of philosophical interest that relate to cosmology and astrophysics.[1] I suspect that the majority of these topics have yet to be mined by philosophers.

---

[1] Smeenk and Ellis (2017) survey debates in philosophy of cosmology, including some topics that have lost prominence today. The Oxford bibliography in philosophy of cosmology (Fox et al., 2019) is a good starting point for further reading. Boyd et al. (2023) collect papers

I will proceed as follows. The remainder of this Introduction will lay down some necessary groundwork: delineating the scope of cosmology, astrophysics, and astronomy, as well as providing some scientific background. The next four sections focus on specific research topics in cosmology and astrophysics: cosmic inflation (Section 2), dark matter (Section 3), dark energy (Section 4), and black holes (Section 5). The first three are examples of novel physics that is introduced primarily on cosmological or astrophysical grounds. And while black holes are a generic prediction of general relativity and therefore not 'properly' novel, they are also areas where novel physics is expected to play a role. For reasons of brevity, I will therefore sometimes refer to all four cases as 'novel physics'. For each case, I recount the most important evidence and review the philosophical questions they raise. As such, all four cases also serve as counterexamples to the idea that cosmology and astrophysics are somehow inherently limited. Section 6 takes a step back to assess the epistemology and ethics of cosmology and astrophysics more generally. Section 7 concludes by highlighting certain themes that reappear throughout the different sections of this Element. Most of these are topics that are of interest to philosophers of science more generally, but that can take on a new flavor in the context of philosophy of cosmology and astrophysics.

1.1 Cosmology, Astrophysics, and Astronomy

Cosmology, astrophysics and astronomy all investigate the universe beyond the boundaries of the solar-system, but with different focuses. While the boundaries between the three disciplines are blurred, a rough delineation of the three will help us to get clearer on the current subject matter (see also Jacquart, 2020, fn. 1).

Cosmology studies the origin and evolution of the universe at the largest scales. It describes how the universe evolved from an initial hot dense state until today, approximately 13.8 billion years later, and how, during that time, the large-scale structure in the universe arose from the formation of the lightest elements to the development of the 'cosmic web', a structure of galaxy clusters and filaments connecting them. As a discipline, relativistic cosmology is approximately 100 years old. Einstein (1917) first applied general relativity to the universe as a whole. However, for the first fifty years or so, the discipline remained largely theoretical, with a limited empirical basis. This changed in 1965 with the discovery of the Cosmic Microwave Background radiation

---

from most leading scholars in philosophy of astrophysics, as well as a comprehensive annotated bibliography (Yetman, 2023).

(CMB), a remnant of the Big Bang that provides a map of our universe when it was very young. Today, cosmologists use large-scale structure surveys, detailed data from the CMB and various other observational probes to test their models of the universe at the largest scales.

Astrophysics describes the evolution of stars, galaxies, galaxy clusters, black holes and other structures in the universe, using the laws of physics. As a discipline, it originated in the nineteenth century, when spectroscopy was first applied to the Sun (Boyd, 2023, 15-16). This work revealed for the first time the applicability of nuclear physics to stellar interiors. Today, astrophysics is extremely broad in scope. It covers an enormous range of objects and scales – from individual molecules in the inter-stellar medium to galaxy clusters. Its primary aim is to offer causal explanations for observations of astrophysical objects. Unlike cosmology, it is not just interested in unique objects, but also in generalizations about types of objects (instead of token examples), from main-sequence stars to spiral galaxies (Anderl, 2016).

Astronomy is primarily a cartographic exercise, mapping out different structures in the sky. It does not primarily concern itself with offering causal explanations based on, for instance, what happens in stellar interiors, although it does offer the observational basis for much of cosmology and astrophysics. It is one of the oldest scientific disciplines, dating back to prehistoric times. Today, we have entered the era of multi-messenger astronomy. Astronomers are no longer confined to a single type of signal, for example, electromagnetic waves in the optical spectrum. Instead, astronomers now study a very broad range of the electromagnetic spectrum, but they also study neutrino signals, gravitational waves, and cosmic rays (Abelson, 2022b).

The three fields don't just differ in subject matter, but also in terms of their philosophical investigation. While cosmology has received fairly consistent attention from philosophers over the last couple of decades, philosophy of astrophysics is a much younger field. And although it is possible that some papers in philosophy of cosmology could qualify as philosophy of astrophysics (e.g., some work in philosophy of dark matter), that is not going to be the case for all. In reality, philosophy of astrophysics and philosophy of astronomy so far, even more so than philosophy of cosmology, remain an untapped mine for philosophy of science.

1.2 Some Scientific Background

Before delving into the philosophical debates, it will be useful to provide some scientific background. The examples of novel physics discussed in Sections 2–4 are deeply connected to ΛCDM ("Lambda Cold Dark Matter"), the current concordance model of cosmology. ΛCDM uses general relativity (GR) in combination with assumptions that the universe is homogeneous ("no special points in spacetime") and isotropic ("no preferred directions") to describe the evolution of the universe. The combined assumptions of homogeneity and isotropy are known as the 'Cosmological Principle' (see Section 6.2.3).

Given the Cosmological Principle, which also implies that the stress-energy tensor is that of a perfect fluid, the universe can be described by an FLRW-metric:

$$ds^2 = -dt^2 + a(t)d\sigma^2 \tag{1}$$

$a(t)$ denotes the (dimensionless) scale factor. It is related to the Hubble parameter, which measures the expansion rate of the universe:

$$H(t) \equiv \frac{\dot{a}(t)}{a(t)} \tag{2}$$

H_0 is the current value for the Hubble parameter. The evolution of the scale factor is described by the Einstein Field Equations, which, thanks to the homogeneity and isotropy assumptions, simplify to the Friedman equations:

$$\left(\frac{\dot{a}}{a}\right)^2 = \frac{8\pi G \rho}{3} - \frac{k}{a^2} + \frac{\Lambda}{3} \tag{3}$$

$$\frac{3\ddot{a}}{a} = -4\pi G (\rho + 3p) + \Lambda \tag{4}$$

In these equations, Λ is the cosmological constant. The curvature is represented by k. $k = 1$ represents a closed universe, $k = -1$ a hyperbolic universe, and $k = 0$ a flat universe, which occurs when the energy density of the universe equals the critical density $\rho_{crit} = \frac{3H^2}{8\pi G}$. ρ and p are the usual density and pressure.

Different contributions to the energy budget of the universe have a different effect on the evolution of the scale factor. This is reflected in their equations of state, that is, relations between pressure and density. The equation-of-state parameter w, defined in the barotropic equation of state as $p = w\rho$, can be used to track how different energy density contributions influence the evolution of the scale factor in the Friedman equations:

$$\rho \propto a^{-3(1+w)} \tag{5}$$

The most important equations of state are those for radiation (neutrinos and photons; $w = 1/3$), matter (baryonic and dark, assumed to be collisionless; $w = 0$), and dark energy ($w = -1$).

FLRW-models offer a first-order description of the evolution of the universe at the largest scales. In order to account for large-scale structure formation, small near-scale-invariant Gaussian primordial density perturbations are introduced. These are detected in the CMB as perturbations of the order of 10^{-5}, but they form the seeds of what through gravitational collapse become galaxies, clusters, and super-clusters. One of the central questions of early-universe cosmology is what formed these primordial density perturbations. The leading answer since the 1980s comes from cosmic inflation (discussed in Section 2).

Over time, it has become clear that in order to describe the evolution of large-scale structure in the universe, the universe must contain more than baryonic matter alone, that is, matter consisting of three quarks, like protons or neutrons. Most matter that humans encounter on a day-to-day basis is baryonic. However, the current energy density budget of the universe also contains approximately 27% dark matter and 69% dark energy, in addition to the 5% baryonic matter (Planck Collaboration, Aghanim, et al. 2020). This is reflected in the name of the current cosmological concordance model: Λ refers to dark energy, CDM to (cold) dark matter. Dark matter (see Section 3) behaves as an additional source of gravitational collapse, while dark energy (see Section 4) is a placeholder term for what causes the accelerated expansion of the universe. Current observations are compatible with the total energy density of the universe equalling the critical density, suggesting that the universe is flat.

The success of ΛCDM as a theory of large-scale structure formation is remarkable. The predictions derived through computer simulations (more on this in Section 6) agree with observations of large-scale structure. Further evidence comes from observations of element abundances corresponding to predictions based on Big Bang Nucleosynthesis, the theory of the formation of the lightest elements in the early universe. It is even more remarkable how quickly this success was achieved: the fact that the universe is larger than the Milky Way was only broadly confirmed in 1925, and the fact that it is expanding became relatively established in the late 1920s and early 1930s (De Baerdemaeker & Schneider, 2022). The first unification between cosmological and astrophysical missing mass (dark matter) did not occur until the 1970s (de Swart, 2020, 2022; de Swart, Bertone, & van Dongen, 2017), cosmic inflation was first proposed in the 1970s and 1980s (Guth, 1981), and the supernova evidence for the accelerated expansion of the universe was discovered in the 1990s.

Arguably the most important source of empirical evidence for cosmology today is the CMB. The CMB provides a snapshot of the universe approximately 380,000 years after the Big Bang. It was formed at recombination, when atomic nuclei and electrons formed neutral atoms, and photons became free-streaming. Since recombination, these photons have been free-streaming throughout the universe. Although shifted to the red because of the universe's expansion, their spectrum has remained unchanged. Penzias and Wilson discovered the CMB in 1965 as an ineliminable background noise in their radio antenna. At the time, this evidence played a crucial role in establishing Big Bang Cosmology over the rival steady-state theory (although see Ćirković & Perović 2018, for nuances to the common narrative). In the 1990s, the COBE satellite allowed scientists to establish for the first time that the CMB had a perfect black-body spectrum. Follow-up satellites WMAP's and Planck's increased sensitivity allowed cosmologists to detect the slight anisotropies in the CMB, and to map out their full power spectrum. Today, the precise values of the six free parameters of the ΛCDM model (aside from the dark matter density and the baryonic matter density also the age of the universe, the scalar spectral index, the curvature fluctuation amplitude, and the reionization optical depth) are determined by the Planck results from the 2010s (Planck Collaboration, Aghanim, et al. 2020).

Given the recent nature of most of what, today, is considered 'established knowledge in cosmology', it should come as no surprise that there are many open questions. Some of them will return in the next sections. What is the nature of dark matter? What causes the accelerated expansion of the universe? And, the focus of the next section, whence the primordial density fluctuations revealed by the CMB?

2 Cosmic Inflation

Given the energy scales of the universe immediately after the Big Bang, the physics governing the early universe is expected to be quite different than that governing the later stages. Cosmologists can very conservatively assume that current theories of particle physics apply to the universe from Big Bang Nucleosynthesis onwards, because the universe had expanded and cooled down sufficiently by that time. But there are no inductive grounds for extrapolations of high-energy physics to some of the earliest eras, and GR is expected to break down at some point in the early universe as well. Unsurprisingly, then, this era presents multiple puzzles (Smeenk, 2017).

One prominent theory for the early universe that purports to explain where the primordial density fluctuations revealed by the CMB originate from is cosmic inflation. Inflation posits that the early universe underwent an era of accelerated expansion. This expansion phase was fueled by a new type of field, the inflaton field (initial speculations that the Higgs field could fuel inflationary expansion were quickly abandoned), of which the behavior is governed by the inflaton potential. At the end of the inflationary phase, the inflaton decayed into the more familiar matter-energy content of the universe which then evolved according to the standard descriptions of ΛCDM. This process is somewhat confusingly referred to as 'reheating'.

Since its inception, inflation received broad acceptance in the cosmology community fairly quickly.[2] Philosophers are still grappling with whether this quick acceptance was epistemically licensed. The main challenge is: how can we confirm a theory of the early universe, given that it posits novel physics and that the empirical access to that early universe is limited to observations of downstream effects? This challenge is complicated by the fact that inflation did not resolve any empirical anomalies for the then-current Hot Big Bang model[3], unlike dark matter and dark energy. There have been two main arguments offered in favor of inflation: inflation solves fine-tuning problems (Section 2.1), and inflation seeds structure formation (Section 2.2). Both of these come with caveats and open questions. Let's take each in turn, before considering some metaphysical implications (Section 2.3).

2.1 The Early Case for Inflation: Fine-Tuning Problems

The original motivation behind inflation was to resolve various fine-tuning problems within our universe (Guth, 1981): the flatness problem, the horizon problem, and the magnetic monopole problem[4]. These problems refer to peculiar features of our universe, that, although not in tension with any physical theory, are so striking that they seem to demand an explanation.

As McCoy (2015) highlights, while it is easy to give a compelling gloss for the flatness and horizon problems, it's much harder to precisely pin down what the explanatory gap exactly is that inflation supposedly fills. For space reasons, I restrict the discussion here to McCoy's intuitively compelling gloss. Readers interested in a more detailed discussion of the fine-tuning problems themselves should turn to McCoy's paper and references therein.

The *flatness problem* refers to the fact that the current spatial curvature of the universe appears to be (nearly) zero. However, zero curvature is an unstable point: even the slightest deviation from flatness would lead to the universe evolving to ever-increasing deviations from flatness. Given its current value, the curvature in the early universe must have been even closer to zero. Inflation

---

[2] Guth (1981) is a milestone in bringing inflation to the general attention of the scientific community, but there were several other scientists preceding this work. See Earman & Mosterín (1999), McCoy (2019) for details on the history of inflation and the quick acceptance of the theory.

[3] The Hot Big Bang model was largely similar to ΛCDM, except for the fact that the cosmological constant Λ was assumed to be zero. This also meant that the energy density of the universe was thought to potentially be much lower.

[4] This problem refers to the lack of observed magnetic monopoles in our universe. It only arises if one accepts Grand Unified Theories and is therefore not a problem for standard Hot Big Bang cosmology (McCoy, 2015). I won't discuss it further here.

would solve this problem because the exponential expansion of space would smooth out any curvature that was present before the inflationary epoch. It would basically reset the universe to close-to-flatness.

The *horizon problem* refers to the remarkable uniformity of the universe as observed in the CMB. This uniformity suggests that the entire observable universe must have been in causal contact to generate this uniformity (e.g., by reaching some thermal equilibrium) before the decoupling of the CMB. Any such process would have required the different regions of the observable universe to be causally connected before recombination. Here's the catch: this is in direct tension with the fact that certain regions of the observable universe have not been in causal contact with one another according to the regular expanding-universe models. Due to the finite speed of light, they fall outside of each other's particle horizons. Without assuming some novel process in the early universe that allowed these regions to be in causal contact, the homogeneity of the CMB could only be explained by uniform initial conditions across the observable universe.

Inflation offers such a novel process. The exponential expansion of space during the inflationary epoch would cause nonuniform regions of space to be stretched beyond the particle horizon scales. The different regions of the CMB were therefore in causal contact before the inflationary epoch. Specifically, they were part of a single region that was in equilibrium before inflation began, and that was stretched out beyond the horizon during inflation. Different parts of that region keep re-entering the horizon after reheating, as the universe continues to expand.

Regardless of the specifics of the fine-tuning problems, one could wonder if a new physical process is necessary to account for them. Couldn't they be solved by referring to the initial conditions of the very early universe? The explanation then is that the universe appears fine-tuned because it had peculiar initial conditions that were evolved forward. After all, many standard explanations in physics combine initial conditions with laws of nature to explain an observed physical state of a system (Earman & Mosterin, 1999; McCoy, 2015).

In cosmology, however, referring to the initial conditions of the universe tends to be unsatisfactory. Pragmatically, initial conditions are something of a dead-end for research (the importance of this pragmatic consideration in theory choice is also highlighted by Wolf & Thébault 2023). They amount to brute facts that need to be accepted at face value. But the early universe is one of the only regimes where we might find observable traces of Planck-scale physics or theories of quantum gravity (Schneider, 2021, 2023). Resorting to initial conditions thus amounts to shutting down an entire research avenue. Relatedly, there is a difference between the initial conditions of the universe and other physical systems: for other physical systems, we can usually explain where the initial conditions come from ('the ball is at the top of the hill at rest because I put it there'). There is no analogue for this in case of the universe – so what explains those initial conditions? Earman and Mosterin (1999) therefore identify the fact that inflation allowed scientists to ask *why*-questions about the early universe as one of the sociological factors leading to its rapid spread. Finally, the initial-conditions route is incomplete because it does not reveal where the initial conditions are supposed to be imposed. At the Planck scale? Earlier? Later? In light of all of this, a dynamical explanation that makes the puzzling features (or the initial conditions) generic (in a way to be specified later) would be at least pragmatically preferable. Inflation purports to offer precisely such a dynamical explanation.

However, pragmatic reasons are not always accepted as grounds for epistemic confirmation. If we reject the initial-conditions explanation based on pragmatic grounds, does that mean that inflation can be epistemically confirmed based on its resolution of fine-tuning problems? There are some reasons to be doubtful.

The fine-tuning problems consist of features of the observable universe that are not prohibited by or in tension with the standard model of cosmology, but that nonetheless strike physicists as 'unlikely', 'surprising' or 'improbable' if their explanation is restricted to specific initial conditions. In other words, there is no strict empirical anomaly that inflation purports to solve here. Rather, the observed flatness and uniformity of the universe require very specific initial conditions, and physicists consider it unlikely that our universe would have exactly those initial conditions out of the much broader set of all possible initial conditions. Inflation supposedly solves the fine-tuning problems by offering a dynamical explanation: the dynamics of inflation are such that the universe, regardless of its initial conditions before inflation took place, would generically lead to a universe with the observed 'surprising' features of our universe.

While intuitively compelling, there are some issues. First, there is the open question whether inflation suffers from an initial conditions problem itself. It is not clear whether all models of inflation can get triggered regardless of the preceding initial conditions (Brandenberger, 2017). Second, McCoy (2015) points out that moving beyond the intuition to pinpoint where the exact problem lies is a difficult task, but this is essential in order for inflation to gain confirmation from solving the fine-tuning problems. To properly consider the fine-tuning problems as 'problems', two questions need to be answered: (i) why are these initial conditions special?; and, (ii) why are such special initial conditions problematic? McCoy finds it plausible that for the flatness and horizon problems, (i) could be answered. The horizon problem could be considered 'special' because it requires some maximal degree of symmetry, for example, while the flatness problem requires a dynamical instability as an initial condition.

But *just* pointing out that the initial conditions of the universe are special is insufficient for them to constitute a *problem*. Sometimes systems just have peculiar initial conditions. As long as these are not in tension with the applicable theory, it's unclear that there is a problem to be solved. What would that require? McCoy sees two possibilities. One reason would be that these special initial conditions are somehow improbable. Making this case requires defining a physically meaningful probability measure (roughly, a function that assigns probability values to all members of a set and with a total value of 1) over all initial conditions. This hasn't been done yet: both defining the space of possibilities, and defining a meaningful probability measure over that space turn out to be nontrivial (see, e.g., McCoy 2017, for a critical take on one candidate measure). At most, this route leads to a promise of a problem, not a formulation of the actual problem, and the road in between is riddled with obstacles.

Another reason to consider the fine-tuning problems genuine anomalies is that the initial conditions are somehow not explanatory in themselves. For instance, Wolf and Thébault (2023) argue that the problematic nature of initial conditions can be cashed out in terms of explanatory depth. But here, McCoy (2015) points out that it is not obvious that special initial conditions are by default not explanatory. As mentioned before, multiple philosophical accounts of explanation, including the deductive-nomological or various causal ones, explicitly include initial conditions in the explanans. It's not clear why the 'specialness' of the initial conditions would make them any less explanatory. Special initial conditions may serve as a guide for future research, but a theory making them generic doesn't imply confirmation.[5]

What does this imply for the status of (classic) inflation? Not much, in the sense that inflation is still consistent with the fine-tuned features of the observable universe. In other words, it doesn't mean that inflation is now a theory in crisis, faced with anomalies. It does mean, however, that while fine-tuning may have been a fine pragmatic motivation, inflation solving fine-tuning problems does not necessarily confer any confirmation of the theory. This is where structure formation comes in.

---

[5] McCoy has recently become more optimistic about fine-tuning problems giving epistemic reasons to accept inflation (McCoy, 2019). Counter to Earman and Mosterin's (1999) sociological take on the early acceptance, McCoy argues that the explanations inflation offered for fine-tuned features provided solid epistemic reasons. However, McCoy recognizes that this argument requires a formulation of the fine-tuning problems in an epistemically salient way, which is only suggested at in the paper.

2.2 The Current Case for Inflation: Structure Formation

Immediately after Guth's seminal paper, a new, much stronger argument for inflation arose. In the 1970s, cosmologists had convened on a phenomenological model for the spectrum of initial density perturbations that provided the seeds for the observed large-scale structure. The Harrison-Peebles-Zel'dovich spectrum is one of small, adiabatic, near-scale-invariant, slightly red-tilted, Gaussian perturbations. But the origin of these perturbations remained unknown. Scientists soon realized that quantum fluctuations in the inflaton field could produce a spectrum with the required properties (Guth & Pi, 1982).

The CMB prediction is still considered the strongest argument in favor of inflation. While the power spectrum, like the horizon and flatness problems, ultimately is an initial-conditions problem, it does provide a more severe test for the predictions of inflation due to the more specific properties of the power spectrum. This empirical success has also been important for the further development of inflation as a theory: as more details about the primordial density perturbations are revealed by better CMB observations, further constraints are placed on the nature of the inflaton field and the shape of the inflaton potential (Planck Collaboration, Akrami, et al. 2020).

Yet, despite this new case in favor of inflation, controversy remains and rivaling theories for the early universe are not counted out. One reason is that inflation's prediction of the CMB power spectrum suffers from the so-called 'trans-Planckian problem', first introduced by Martin and Brandenberger (2001). The trans-Planckian problem boils down to a failure of separation of scales, such that modes at and beyond the Planck scale become relevant for the prediction of the power spectrum.[6]

Another reason is that there is disagreement about what requirements should be imposed on a theory of the early universe and how well inflation satisfies them. As we will see next, many of the discussions implicitly or explicitly draw on Popper's work on the demarcation problem, according to which falsifiability is a necessary property of any scientific theory. Moreover, Popper admonished the use of ad hoc changes to scientific theories in order to accommodate recalcitrant data. It turns out, however, that the line between novel prediction and mere accommodation is difficult to draw in context of inflationary cosmology.

The disagreement about the scientific status of inflation came to a head in 2017, when in the pages of *Scientific American* two camps were battling about the status of inflation as a scientific hypothesis (Guth et al., 2017;

---

[6] See Schneider (2021), Wolf & Thébault (2023) for philosophical discussions.

Ijjas, Steinhardt, & Loeb, 2017).[7] Several charges were brought against inflation, the most scathing one that inflation is not falsifiable (or generally untestable) and therefore not scientific. Thus, despite its empirical success, it is worthwhile to examine the nature of inflation as a scientific theory in more detail. What grounds this criticism of unfalsifiability?

2.2.1 Eternal Inflation

One major stimulus for the charges that the theory is unscientific, is that the theory of inflation has seen some interesting developments. The short nontechnical introduction at the beginning of this section was most faithful to Guth's original proposal. In the past forty years, however, the development of this idea has brought some peculiar features to the fore.

First is the idea that inflation may lead to so-called eternal inflation. This is sometimes called a 'generic' result of inflation, although Smeenk (2014) points out that qualitative suggestions for the mechanism behind eternal inflation are not easily made more precise. Regardless, the basic idea is that globally, inflation continues indefinitely, while it may end locally in regions that subsequently become causally closed off from one another and effectively form pocket universes. And because inflation continues globally, it is to be expected that there are infinitely many pocket universes, all with possibly different parameter values from our universe for fundamental constants, mass densities, and so on. As Guth put it:

> [In] an eternally inflating universe, anything that can happen will happen; in fact, it will happen an infinite number of times. Thus, the question of what is possible becomes trivial – anything is possible, unless it violates some absolute conservation law. (Guth, 2007, 6819)

Our universe then becomes just one in an infinite ensemble of universes that can be extremely similar, but also extremely different from ours. What does that imply for the predictive power of inflation?

Critics of inflation consider this situation rather dire – Ijjas et al. (2017, 39) refer to the inflationary multiverse as a "multimess". Defenders of inflation are more hopeful. Guth himself already highlights the crucial element in the continuation of the quote above: "To extract predictions from the theory, we must therefore learn to distinguish the probable from the improbable" (Guth, 2007, 6819). The idea is the following. Because the inflationary multiverse predicts that "anything can happen", the theory can no longer be assessed based on specific predictions that one thing will happen rather than another. The next best thing is to assess what the parameter values are that the theory predicts will

---

[7] See Dawid & McCoy (2023) for a philosophical reconstruction of the debate and for references preceding the 2017 papers.

generically be observed – what a 'typical observer' in the multiverse would expect to observe for their pocket universe. If a typical observer is expected to observe a universe like ours, then the predictions of eternal inflation are still borne out despite the fact that we live in an infinite multiverse.

Smeenk (2014) shows this is no easy task. There needs to be a probability distribution across the different pocket universes in order to be able to make any probabilistic statements. This brings us back to the measure problem: defining such a probability distribution requires a well-defined ensemble with an appropriate probability measure defined on it. But the ensemble of pocket universes is infinite, and there is no consensus on an appropriate measure on the inflationary multiverse. Even if such a measure could be found, it is not obvious that that permits probabilistic assessments for a 'typical observer': the link between measure and probability distribution needs to be argued for.

Now, one may think that the measure problem does not have to be a fatal blow to the predictive power of eternal inflation. If physicists come up with an appropriate measure and probability distribution, eternal inflation would be predictive once more. Norton (2021) believes that this is doubtful. Norton argues that one cannot assume that the uncertainty in the theory of eternal inflation can be represented probabilistically – this depends on the specifics of the theory (or, in Norton's words, on "background facts"). In the case of inflation, the background facts do not warrant a probabilistic representation of the 'chanciness' of a universe like ours in the inflationary multiverse. Rather, the logic of an infinite lottery applies. Unfortunately for eternal inflation, the predictive power of the inductive logic of infinite lotteries is not as strong as that of probabilistic logic. This is because, according to Norton, "virtually all possible distributions of the properties [like our universe] and [unlike our universe] are assigned equal chance" (2021, S3867). When it comes to arguing that our universe is 'generic' or 'expected', the infinite lottery logic doesn't solve eternal inflation's prediction problem.

Does the lack of an appropriate measure mean that eternal inflation is lost in a 'multimess' for good? Not necessarily. Guth et al. (2017, 6) claim that:

> If the multiverse picture is valid, then the Standard Model would be properly understood as a description of the physics in our visible universe, and similarly the models of inflation that are being refined by current observations would describe the ways inflation can happen in our particular part of the universe.

One way to make sense of this is to remember the successful predictions inflation made for the CMB.[8] This was an empirical prediction of the

---

[8] I'm indebted to Richard Dawid for this point.

framework for our observable universe. While inflation cannot predict the parameter values observed in our universe without a measure, it can still be predictive for other features of the universe, and remain silent on what happens in a 'generic universe'.

2.2.2 Models and Theory

Of course, inflation can only hope to make predictions for our universe if the theory is sufficiently specific. This leads me to a second issue: the fact that the theoretical framework of inflation is very permissive with regards to the inflaton field and the shape of the inflaton potential. Guth originally believed that the inflaton field could be the then-not-yet-found Higgs field, but this idea was quickly rebutted. The inflaton field is a novel type of scalar field, its behavior primarily constrained by it having to generate the CMB power spectrum.

CMB observations have constrained the permitted models to now favor so-called slow-roll inflation. Slow-roll inflation posits that the inflaton field began its evolution on a plateau of the potential, after which it slowly rolled down to oscillate around a minimum. But even within slow-roll inflation, the permitted parameter space is fairly large. In their seminal textbook on the early universe, Kolb and Turner (1990, 313) therefore refer to inflation as "a paradigm in search of a model".

Dawid and McCoy (2023) show that the model-flexibility of inflationary cosmology lies at the heart of the high-profile scientific dispute in the 2010s. The main criticism on inflation from Ijjas et al. (2014, 2017) is that inflation is not testable due to its flexibility:

> [T]he expected outcome of inflation can easily change if we vary the initial conditions, change the shape of the inflationary energy density curve, or simply note that it leads to eternal inflation and a multimess. Individually and collectively, these features make inflation so flexible that no experiment can ever disprove it. (Ijjas et al., 2017, 39)

Because the model space of inflation is so ill-constrained, any model that gets excluded will not affect the status of cosmic inflation as a theory. Ijjas et al. argue that the untestability of the inflationary theory, despite the testability of individual models, implies that cosmic inflation is at odds with the scientific method.

Unsurprisingly, this (implicit) claim of unscientificality played a large role in sparking a response from scientists working on inflation. Calling cosmic inflation unscientific dismisses the work of hundreds of good-faith scientists. In response to the criticism of untestability, defenders of inflation argue that "the testability of a theory in no way requires that all its predictions be independent of the choice of parameters" (Guth et al., 2017). In other words, the claimed flexibility in terms of initial conditions and inflaton potentials is no different from the flexibility awarded to many other theories of physics (after all, the Standard Model of particle physics also has nineteen free parameters).

Dawid and McCoy (2023) analyze this disagreement in terms of different views on theory testing. Both critics and defenders of cosmic inflation agree that inflation is empirically adequate with regard to the CMB data. The disagreement, however, is about whether or not that empirical adequacy is due to mere ad hoc accommodation. Dawid and McCoy identify the criticism of Ijjas et al. with a strict view on testability: the theory needs to be fully specified before empirical testing can take place. If the theory has not been fully specified, it implies that its empirical adequacy is due to accommodation.

Defenders of inflation disagree. Dawid and McCoy see this defense as reflective of a more process-based view on theory development and testing, where comparing models of a theory with data can be part of specifying the theory. In particular, due to the unfamiliar regime where inflationary cosmology took place and due to the inflaton being a novel field, there are limited theoretical constraints on inflation. It is therefore unsurprising that scientists search for empirical guidance. The extensive model building and subsequent testing of models is part of an effort to develop inflationary theory. Inflation is, in other words, in a "constructive phase of eliminative reasoning" (Dawid & McCoy, 2023, 14), rather than a phase of ad hoc accommodation. The goal of that constructive phase is not picking out 'the' correct model of inflation, but rather to develop the theory and ultimately ground inflationary cosmology in fundamental physics. According to this defense, it is too early to pass a final verdict on inflation, and it is unclear when that final verdict will be appropriate.

This response raises a new question for Dawid and McCoy: at which point has the constructive phase gone on for too long? In other words, at what point is it no longer justified to pursue a theory without having good reason to believe the theory is promising? Dawid and McCoy suggest that there is an epistemic case to be made for the current significant trust in the viability of inflation as a theory in terms of meta-empirical theory assessment. However, Wolf (2024) argues that the meta-empirical case for inflation fails due to the lack of a meta-inductive argument. And while Smeenk (2019) agrees with Dawid and McCoy on a long-term assessment of scientific theories, Smeenk argues against the pursuitworthiness of inflation due to its departure from particle physics and the troubles with eternal inflation.

2.2.3 Early-Universe Cosmology as a Historical Science

It is clear from the previous section that the last word has not been said about the status of cosmic inflation. This is in large part due to the peculiar epistemic context in which early-universe cosmology takes place. One salient aspect I want to reflect on further is that early-universe research aims to reconstruct the deep past based on limited contemporary observations of relics of that past. This is reminiscent of historical sciences more generally, that is, scientific fields that are aimed at reconstructing the deep past, like archeology or paleontology.

According to Cleland (2002) (see also Anderl 2016), stereotypical historical science tends to rely on 'smoking gun'-type reasoning. The idea is the following: in historical sciences, scientists only have access to traces, that is, the outcomes of a causal chain, and they have to rely on those traces to reconstruct that causal chain. Given a set of local traces, historical scientists can hypothesize explanations that unify that set under one causal story. Since there would often be more than one possible explanation, local underdetermination would need to be broken through so-called 'smoking guns', trace observations that discriminate between the competing hypotheses.

This image of historical sciences has been nuanced by Currie (2015, 2018), who argues that historical sciences are "methodological omnivores" and rely on "investigative scaffolding". Methodological omnivory refers to the fact that scientists will use any method available to them to generate independent lines of evidence for their chosen target, over and above the available traces. This can range from using analogue models and computer simulations to reconstructing a particular causal context as closely as possible. Investigative scaffolding refers to the fact that scientists often only realize that certain evidence is relevant to their research of a particular target once they have generated an initial crude model of that target. That model then becomes a jumping-off point for further research. Because the methodology of historical sciences is much richer than often recognized, Currie believes that we can generally be optimistic about the epistemic potential of these disciplines.

I am generally sympathetic to this broadened image of historical sciences. However, there are features of early-universe cosmology that prohibit the kind of methodological omnivory and investigative scaffolding described by Currie. The possibility of methodological omnivory requires a solid theoretical basis. It is only possible to generate empirical evidence that is relevant to the deep past if one can assume that that evidence is representative of that deep past. For example, Kon-Tiki experiments, contemporary reenactments of past sea voyages (Novick et al., 2020), are only epistemically fruitful because there is sufficient theoretical knowledge about where islands are located, how weather patterns have changed over time, and what materials were available for sea vessels. Similarly, investigative scaffolding requires a starting point to build the scaffold on.

This theoretical basis is lacking in the case of early-universe cosmology. As mentioned before, there is little theoretical guidance for physics in the early universe. Indeed, in defense of inflation, Guth, Kaiser, and Nomura (2014, 113) state that it is "totally inappropriate to judge inflation on how well it fits with anybody's speculative ideas about Planck-scale physics", and they continue that it is hard to assess what assumptions may be "reasonable" between inflationary and Planck-scale physics. In other words, the energy scales in the early universe are so far removed from the scales where current theories of physics apply, that we can't rely on those theories as inductive grounds for inferences about the early universe. It is therefore also not obvious how we could plausibly 'recreate' the early universe conditions in a laboratory today.[9]

What does this imply for the early-universe cosmology? The two factors above seem to severely limit the available epistemic resources. This further implies that Currie's (2018) optimism about the epistemology of historical sciences may not easily extend to early-universe cosmology in the sense that, although cosmologists have been able to develop many how-possibly scenarios about the early universe, the available tools to discriminate between them are limited. It should therefore not be surprising that what Dawid and McCoy call the constructive phase of inflationary cosmology is still ongoing with no clear end in sight.

Does this mean that early-universe cosmology is forever doomed to model-building and how-possibly scenarios? Not necessarily. Every model or theory that gets eliminated based on CMB observations is a step towards better understanding the early universe. Moreover, there is still an inferential strategy available that could lead to faster progress: Cleland's smoking-gun-type reasoning. For example, the failure to detect strong deviations from Gaussianity in the 2013 Planck data release meant a significant blow to the so-called ekpyrotic universe models, an alternative to inflation (Planck Collaboration et al., 2014). Similarly, primordial gravitational waves could provide strong evidence in favor of inflation, although the case is more complicated than is commonly suggested (Brandenberger, 2019). Thus, if a smoking gun for inflation can be found, there will be good reason to prefer inflation over other scenarios for the early universe, and vice versa.

---

[9] A similar concern will return in context of analogue black hole experiments, discussed in Section 5.3.

2.3 Multiverse Realism

To conclude the discussion of early-universe cosmology, I want to briefly turn to scientific realism and inflation. Scientific realism in general is a commitment to the (approximate) truth of our best scientific theories, and therefore also to the existence of the observables and unobservables they posit (Chakravartty, 2017). The realism question about the inflationary multiverse has not been discussed in the philosophical literature so far, but that should not be surprising: it may seem preemptive to discuss the metaphysical implications of inflation before the theory itself is developed and further confirmed. And indeed, given the preceding analysis, it seems premature to commit to belief in the existence of the inflationary multiverse, regardless of one's tendencies elsewhere. Nonetheless, it is worthwhile to look at inflation as a peculiar test case for scientific realism.

Let us suppose that a smoking gun is found in favor of inflation and the scientific consensus grows further that inflation is indeed a successful theory of the early universe. What does this imply for the scientific realist? Is she now committed to accepting the reality of the inflationary multiverse? In other words, is she now committed to accepting that, as Guth put it, anything that can happen will happen an infinite number of times?

Let me explain why inflation presents a puzzle for the realist debate.[10] Any empirical confirmation of inflation would necessarily come from observations within our universe. Inflation generically implies eternal inflation, according to which our universe is just one in an infinite multiverse, but where we are causally closed off from every other pocket universe. This is what makes the case peculiar: the theory explicitly precludes any causal chain that bridges between other pocket universes and our own universe. That makes it different from, say, subatomic particles: while those are inaccessible to our naked eyes because of the associated length scales, there is a realist case to be made that we can track the causal effects of these subatomic particles to observed detector signals. It also makes it different from extinct organisms, which are empirically inaccessible because of the associated time scales. Based on the fossil record, it is still possible to construct a causal inference from the fossil record to the now-extinct organism that would suffice to warrant a realist commitment. In contrast, CMB observations may permit a causal inference from primordial gravitational waves to the once-existence of an inflaton field and its associated inflationary

---

[10] I am indebted to Nora Boyd for informal discussions of this puzzle.

phase in the early universe. But does commitment to an inflationary phase in the evolution of *our* universe automatically imply a commitment to the existence of the inflationary multiverse – a different causal effect of the inflaton field, distinct from the primordial gravitational waves?

It seems to me that several versions of selective scientific realism would be hesitant about this inference. These views are only committed to realism about specific parts of our current best scientific theories, thus leaving room for theory change without this theory change affecting the realist commitment. For example, the explanationist realist along the lines of Psillos (1999) is committed to the existence of those entities that are indispensable to explaining the predictive success of a scientific theory. It is not immediately clear whether the multiverse is indispensable in such a way, since it seems more like an unwanted side-effect than an essential component of inflation. Entity realists (e.g., Hacking 1983) are committed to realism about entities to the extent that they can manipulate them to bring about other effects. They would likely be hesitant about commitment to the multiverse because of the lack of causal access to it. These examples suggest that commitment to the multiverse is not a necessary consequence of a broader realist commitment to inflation.

3 Dark Matter

Aside from inflation, there are two more examples of genuinely novel physics proposed in cosmology, that is, physics that falls beyond the scope of the combination of the standard model of high-energy physics and general relativity. One of these is called dark energy (discussed in the next section), the other dark matter. Together, they are responsible for 95% of the current energy density of the universe.

Dark matter is nonbaryonic, meaning that it cannot be constituted by particles made up of three quarks, it is electromagnetically close-to-neutral, and slow-moving in context of large-scale structure formation (Workman et al., 2022). Standard-Model neutrinos can make up a small fraction of dark matter in the universe, but they don't qualify as slow-moving (in other words as 'cold' dark matter) and are therefore usually treated as a separate contribution to the energy density of the universe in addition to baryonic matter and cold dark matter. The vast majority of the dark matter in our universe has to be constituted by something novel, be it primordial black holes or Beyond-the-Standard-Model particles. Despite its elusive nature, there is ample evidence today supporting dark matter's existence. I will first rehearse some of that evidence before delving into its philosophical implications.

3.1 The Case for Dark Matter

At galaxy scales, Rubin's observations of flat galaxy rotation curves were ground-breaking (Rubin & Ford, 1970). Assuming the observed mass distribution of luminous matter, Newtonian dynamics (the applicable approximation to GR on galaxy scales) predicts that the rotational velocity of stars will fall off with increasing distance from the galactic center. But Rubin observed that the velocity of stars remained more or less constant, regardless of their distance from the center. The rotation curves, which plot rotational velocity in function of distance from the galactic center, were therefore called 'flat'. One way of accounting for these observations is by modifying the assumed mass distribution in the galaxy: instead of only taking into account the luminous matter, one could introduce an additional, nonluminous mass source, that is, dark matter.

At cluster scales, both velocity dispersions and gravitational lensing provide evidence for the presence of additional nonluminous matter. In the 1930s, Zwicky (2009/1933) determined the dispersion of galaxy velocities in the Coma Cluster, that is, the spread of velocities of galaxies around the mean. Zwicky found that the dispersion was large, too large for the Coma Cluster to be held together by the gravitational pull of the luminous matter alone. By assuming the presence of nonluminous matter, the stability of the Coma Cluster as a gravitational system can be accounted for, despite the large velocity dispersion.

Much more recently, observations of the Bullet Cluster were touted in the paper title (!) as "a direct empirical proof" for the existence of dark matter (Clowe et al., 2006). The Bullet Cluster is actually a collision event between two galaxy clusters, where one resembles a bullet moving through the other – hence the name. The observers used X-ray observations to determine the distribution of luminous matter. They mapped out the gravitational mass distribution using strong gravitational lensing of background galaxies by the Bullet Cluster. The two did not line up with one another. Clowe et al. concluded that there must be some additional, nonluminous gravitating matter present to account for this misalignment.[11]

Finally, at cosmic scales, the success of ΛCDM as a model of large-scale structure formation crucially depends on positing the existence of cold dark matter. One line of evidence comes from the CMB. The CMB power spectrum

---

[11] There was some philosophical disagreement as to what exactly the Bullet Cluster showed, given that previous inferences to the presence of dark matter assumed general relativity (Kosso, 2013; Sus, 2014; Vanderburgh, 2003, 2005). Vanderburgh (2014) argues that while the Bullet Cluster establishes that dark matter is present, it does not fully break the underdetermination between GR and modified theories of gravity.

is differently sensitive to the presence of dark matter and baryonic matter. The third peak in particular puts tight constraints on the dark matter density Ω_{DM} (Planck Collaboration, Aghanim, et al. 2020). Other evidence comes from Baryonic Acoustic Oscillations (BAOs), that is, oscillations in the matter density in the universe as a result of counteracting influence of gravitational collapse and outward radiation pressure (Eisenstein et al., 2005). They are detectable as a preferential length scale at which galaxies are separated from one another. Because dark matter is only subject to gravitational collapse and not to radiation pressure, it contributes to stronger galaxy formation than what would be the result of baryonic matter alone. Similar lines of evidence also come from Big Bang Nucleosynthesis and from large-scale structure formation. In all cases, explaining the observations requires more gravitating and otherwise minimally interacting matter present than what baryonic matter can account for.

The cosmological and astrophysical case for dark matter is clearly strong. Nonetheless, many candidates remain as far as dark matter constituents are concerned, ranging from primordial black holes over supersymmetric partners to axions. Many hope that dark matter will provide a window on physics Beyond the Standard Model of particle physics, but as of yet, this has not been substantiated. This is not just a scientific problem, but also a philosophical one. Epistemically, there is a question of how to make progress on dark matter research, given that it constitutes genuinely novel physics (Section 3.3). Metaphysically, it is not obvious whether the scientific realist should be committed to the existence of dark matter (Section 3.4). But first, let me turn to a different question, one that the majority of philosophy of dark matter has focused on so far: is there a genuine underdetermination between positing the existence of dark matter and modifying Newtonian dynamics?

3.2 A Peculiar Philosophical Focus

The current scientific consensus is that dark matter makes up approximately 27% of the current energy density of the universe and that there generally is about five times as much nonbaryonic cold dark matter in the universe as there is baryonic matter. Nonetheless, a significant part of the philosophical literature on dark matter centers around whether or not there is genuine underdetermination between two scientific hypotheses: dark matter and MOND – short for Modified Newtonian Dynamics[12] (see, e.g., Jacquart 2021; Martens et al. 2022; Massimi 2018). Indeed, some papers go as far as suggesting that MOND is 'preferable' over dark matter, counter to the scientific

---

[12] See Famaey & McGaugh (2012) for a favorable scientific review of the MOND proposal and its potential relativistic extensions.

consensus (see, e.g., McGaugh 2015; Merritt 2017, 2020, 2021; Milgrom 2020). This raises an obvious question: do the philosophical arguments in favor of MOND hold? Answering this question affirmatively could have significant implications: it would imply that the strong scientific consensus is misguided.

MOND was developed in the early 1980s by Milgrom. To understand its original appeal, it's important to note that the empirical case for dark matter was not as strong then as it is today: several of the key observations that are now rehearsed as evidence for dark matter date post-2000. In fact, the dark matter hypothesis itself only gained traction in the 1970s. de Swart, Bertone, and van Dongen (2017) (see also de Swart 2022) argue that a crucial step in the acceptance of dark matter came in 1974, when two papers were published back-to-back on large-scale structure formation (Einasto, Kaasik, and Saar 1974; Ostriker, Peebles, and Yahil 1974). For the first time, these papers brought together observations from large-scale structure formation, velocity dispersions in clusters, and galaxy rotation curves to argue for the existence of dark matter. The observational evidence was complemented with a theoretical argument: dark matter was necessary to 'close the universe', and a closed universe was at the time preferred on aesthetic grounds. CMB evidence or the Bullet Cluster observations were not available in the 1970s or 1980s. This means that although there was already a good case for cold dark matter in the 1980s, when Milgrom proposed MOND, the case was not quite closed.

Milgrom proposed MOND largely in response to the anomalous flat rotation curves (Bekenstein & Milgrom, 1984; Milgrom, 1983a, 1983b, 1983c). Recall that dark matter accounted for the flat rotation curves by changing the assumed mass distribution. Milgrom's proposal was to keep the mass distribution intact, but to change the governing dynamical laws. In other words, Newtonian dynamics was modified on galactic scales – hence the name MOND.

Today, MOND has largely been discredited by the majority of scientists. There are multiple reasons. First, as discussed before, the empirical case for dark matter is significantly stronger today than it was in the 1980s. In contrast, while MOND has been successful describing phenomenological correlations on galaxy scales, it struggles to account for phenomena on cluster and cosmological scales. This is related to the second reason: there is no broadly accepted relativistic extension of MOND that can replace general relativity and its empirical successes.[13] Worse still, MOND requires changing tried and tested

---

[13] See Abelson (2022a) for a philosophical take on how the LIGO/Virgo-observations of a binary neutron star merger were incompatible with TeVeS, a bi-metric theory that was long considered the most promising relativistic version of MOND.

dynamical laws at one, seemingly arbitrary scale. Meanwhile, dark matter requires no modification of fundamental theories of physics and it is compatible with the presumed incompleteness of the Standard Model of particle physics.

But despite these scientific arguments, several philosophical defenses of MOND have been mounted. Richard Dawid and I have summarized and critically evaluated the three most common types of argument (De Baerdemaeker & Dawid, 2022). The rest of this section draws on that analysis.

First, defenders of MOND appeal to Popper's demarcation criterion of falsifiability. They argue that dark matter as part of ΛCDM is unscientific because ΛCDM is unfalsifiable. This is because predictions from ΛCDM have to be derived through complex computer simulations. Especially for galaxy- or cluster-scales, these simulations tend to include a large swath of free parameters to model nongravitational interactions (at the largest scales, gravity is dominant, significantly reducing the required complexity). As a result, defenders of MOND claim that just about anything can be predicted with those simulations, or, in other words, that these simulations are unfalsifiable.

Second, defenders of MOND argue that the dark matter hypothesis itself is unfalsifiable as long as there is no specific dark matter candidate identified as the sole constituent of dark matter. Without such a specification of 'the' dark matter candidate, any failure to detect a given dark matter candidate with a targeted experiment can just be explained away by arguing that the searched-for candidate does not in fact constitute dark matter. For example, the lack of empirical success for supersymmetry has put pressure on the idea that the lightest supersymmetric partner is a good dark matter candidate, but the dark matter hypothesis itself has not been affected by this result.

Finally, defenders of MOND offer a positive argument in favor of MOND. This positive argument appeals to Lakatos' view on theory change. According to Lakatos, scientific research programs are progressive as long as they successfully make novel predictions, including after modifications to account for previously recalcitrant evidence. They are degenerative if the modifications that are required to accommodate new observations do not lead to novel predictions. Defenders of MOND argue that MOND, unlike dark matter, has made many risky predictions for galaxy-scale phenomenology, for example the Baryonic Tully-Fisher relation or the Radial Acceleration Relation. These predictions have all been borne out by observations. Thus, MOND is a progressive research program: based on a small set of assumptions, it has successfully made several novel predictions.

There are questions to be raised about the scientific basis for these arguments. But even setting those aside, we show that there is a basic philosophical issue with framing any defense of MOND in terms of Lakatosian or Popperian views on theory assessment (De Baerdemaeker & Dawid, 2022, §4). Defenders of MOND aim to make an epistemic claim that MOND is confirmed by its predictive successes and furthermore, that MOND is additionally confirmed by the failure of its only rival, dark matter. This stands in clear tension with the philosophical views they employ. Popper's claims about falsifiability were normative: scientists should not construct unfalsifiable theories. Popper found any notion of credence or confirmation of a scientific theory misguided – but this is exactly what defenders of MOND aim to establish. And Lakatos' work should be understood as a descriptive analysis of the history of science. In other words, it is backward-looking. Lakatos gave no criteria for determining whether an ongoing research program is progressive or degenerative. Using either view for epistemic arguments is therefore a category mistake.[14]

I therefore conclude that the philosophical arguments in favor of MOND are so far unconvincing, in line with the scientific consensus. This also raises a methodological concern about philosophy of dark matter so far. From the perspective of philosophy of science in practice, I find the focus on a debate that is largely absent from the scientific literature to be a missed opportunity. To be sure, there is interesting conceptual work to be done in comparing the conceptual basis of MOND and dark matter (see, e.g., Martens & Lehmkuhl 2020a, 2020b), and the debate can be a useful test case for philosophical views on modeling and theories (see, e.g., Jacquart 2021; Massimi 2018). Explicitly arguing counter to the scientific consensus that there is genuine underdetermination or reason to accept a rival theory, however, comes with a high burden of proof – one that hasn't been met so far. And perhaps it is worthwhile for philosophers interested in dark matter to spend their efforts elsewhere, given how much of dark matter research is as of yet unexplored. The remainder of this section can hopefully give a nudge in that direction.

3.3 Searching for Dark Matter

Perhaps the central question in contemporary dark matter research is: what constitutes dark matter? This question presents a unique challenge. Despite the strong astrophysical and cosmological evidence for dark matter as well as its gravitational behavior (a perfect collisionless fluid), there is very little guidance as to its nongravitational behavior. As Weatherall (2021) points out, that may be because, if dark matter is constituted by primordial black holes, we already

---

[14] That being said, we further argue that it is possible to recast the MONDian defense in epistemic terms by appealing to meta-empirical theory assessment. However, we show that the MONDian defense still fails by those standards (De Baerdemaeker & Dawid, 2022, §5-6).

know everything there is to know about it. Nevertheless, the question stands: how can we know that dark matter is constituted by primordial black holes, or axions, or any other candidate? In other words, how can scientists make progress on learning more about dark matter's nongravitational behavior (including, in a worst-case scenario, that it *only* interacts gravitationally), given that there are so little constraints on that nongravitational behavior?

Given that many dark matter search experiments are underway, making such progress must not be hopeless. Some searches are so-called production experiments: they look for signatures of produced (hence the name) dark matter particles at high-energy colliders like the LHC. Others are direct detection searches with enormous detector vats. They aim to detect a scattering event where a dark matter particle from the Milky Way halo deposits some energy to a waiting atomic nucleus, similar to how solar neutrinos were first discovered. Still others are indirect detection experiments. Unlike direct detection experiments, they don't look for signatures of dark matter scattering off a standard-model particle. Rather, they appeal to the fact that if dark matter is a particle, it is possible that in dark-matter-rich environments (e.g., in the galactic center), dark matter particles might annihilate into standard-model particles, resulting in a detectable signal. Indirect searches look for those signals.[15,16]

Interestingly enough, many experiments searching for dark matter candidates tend to use tried-and-tested technology from high-energy physics. Particle colliders had long proven their success before they explicitly started to focus on dark matter searches. Direct detection experiments were explicitly modeled on the detection methods for solar neutrinos (De Baerdemaeker, 2021, 136-139). This is quite peculiar, since one of the few things that is broadly accepted about what constitutes dark matter is that it cannot be standard model particle physics. So how can these experiments legitimately claim to be searching for dark matter?

I have argued that the structure of justification for new physics searches takes a different form than most other experiments (De Baerdemaeker, 2021). Let me illustrate by contrasting the justification for dark matter experiments with a more typical example: MRI research. Scientists use MRIs to study brain

---

[15] This terminology is the scientific jargon. To what extent the differences between these three types of searches have any epistemic implications, has not yet been explored in the philosophical literature to my knowledge. I want to pre-emptively warn the reader, however, to not draw parallels with the use of "direct" or "indirect" in context of black hole astrophysics, where there is a clear epistemic implication (Section 5). The case of calling the Bullet Cluster "direct evidence" for dark matter seems at face value intended to be more in line with the use of "direct" in black hole astrophysics, but, again, whether this holds has not yet been argued philosophically.

[16] Antoniou (2023, § 3) gives a more comprehensive summary of dark matter searches, including both searches for dark matter candidates and cosmological and astrophysical probes.

structure and other soft tissues in the human body. MRIs use strong magnetic fields that interact with protons in the tissue of interest. Based on differences in alignment times with the magnetic field and in energy releases, scientists can differentiate between different types of tissues.[17] Why do scientists believe that MRI scans are an effective way to map out brain structure? Because they know that the human body consists of different types of tissue and those different types of tissue are constituted by atoms which contain protons. That's it. That very basic knowledge about the human body is sufficient to establish that MRI scans are an appropriate method to detect different brain structures, tumors, or injuries.

The problem with setting up dark matter search experiments is that that very basic knowledge, the analogue of the fact that the human body contains protons, is largely lacking. After all, there are no established properties of dark matter that can give scientists guidance as to which methods may be able to detect the nongravitational behavior of dark matter particles. All we have is gravity, and limits on dark matter's nongravitational behavior.

So how are these dark matter searches justified? The justification follows a different structure, where scientists assume what features dark matter would need to have in order for tried-and-tested experimental setups to be able to detect dark matter particles. Once again, consider an example. As mentioned before, a lot of dark matter direct detection searches were modeled on successful neutrino detection experiments. They are (roughly – I'm setting aside many details here, see De Baerdemaeker (2021, 136-137) for a more complete reconstruction) justified in the following way:

P1: Direct detection experiments like those used for neutrino detection use the weak coupling to detect extraterrestrial particles by their deposited energy in scattering events.

P2: If dark matter is constituted by weakly interacting particles with an appropriate mass, then direct detection experiments like those used for neutrino detection can be used to search for signatures of dark matter particles from the galactic halo.

P3: Given current knowledge about dark matter based on cosmology and astrophysics, it is possible that dark matter is constituted by weakly interacting particles with an appropriate mass.

C: Direct detection experiments like those used for neutrino detection can be used to search for signatures of dark matter particles from the galactic halo.

---

[17] For more details, see this web page from the NIH: https://www.nibib.nih.gov/science-education/science-topics/magnetic-resonance-imaging-mri.

Notice that this kind of 'method-driven' justification requires that the assumptions about dark matter's weak interaction and its mass range are physically permitted given existing knowledge about dark matter (P3), even if there is no positive evidence for it. But even when strong evidence is lacking, the epistemic situation can sometimes be improved through plausibility arguments. In the case of several direct detection experiments, for instance, that plausibility argument comes in the form of the WIMP miracle: the fact that for WIMPs (Weakly Interacting Massive Particles), a popular class of dark matter candidates that also includes supersymmetric particles, the theoretically predicted dark matter abundance precisely matches the observed dark matter abundance.

This structure of justification should raise an obvious concern: doesn't this make the results of dark matter searches dangerously dependent on the assumed properties? Of course, the method-driven justification of dark matter experiments lies on a spectrum with the 'usual' justification for experiments like MRIs, where the location on the spectrum depends on how well the required assumptions for the experiments can be independently justified. It seems that in the case of dark matter searches, these assumptions create an additional hurdle to establishing the reliability of experimental results for dark matter.

A common response to such model-dependence of experimental results is to use robustness arguments: if multiple independent (but model-dependent) results all agree on a measured parameter, this is taken as a good reason to believe that the result is a reliable measurement of the parameter in question. Antoniou (2023) shows, however, that robustness arguments have limited power in dark matter searches for two reasons. First, there is very little overlap between methods that are searching for the same dark matter candidate – in other words, most dark matter searches don't even purport to probe the same parameter. Even when they probe the same parameter, different methods often probe different regions of parameter space, thus still not warranting robustness arguments. Second, the assumptions made in different dark matter searches are mostly about highly specific dark matter candidates and their specific features. That means that results can't be compared across searches for different candidates (as Antoniou puts it, constraining the mass of WIMPs is very different than constraining that of axions). Antoniou concludes that although robustness arguments can be used to increase confidence in results for specific dark matter candidates, they are mostly useless in building up constraints for the overarching dark matter concept.

In light of this limitation on dark matter searches, one could take a different approach and aim to improve the constraints from cosmology and astrophysics on the space of possibilities of dark matter candidates. This can happen through more detailed astrophysical and cosmological observations. The Bullet Cluster, for instance, was crucial in setting some limits on interaction strengths. Similarly, the behavior of dark matter on galactic and sub-galactic scales within the framework of ΛCDM is not yet well-understood. Making progress on how dark matter behaves on smaller scales could provide an important clue for what candidates can constitute dark matter.

But just like with dark matter candidate searches, caution is key. Deriving predictions from ΛCDM for (sub-)galactic scales has to rely on complex computer simulations, since gravity is no longer the sole dominant interaction in this regime. This makes establishing the reliability of simulation outputs all the more challenging (more on this in Section 6). In fact, there are several discrepancies between what cosmological simulations predict, and what is observed: the so-called 'small-scale challenges' for ΛCDM (see, e.g., Bullock & Boylan-Kolchin 2017, for a review). While it has sometimes been argued that these small-scale challenges provide motivation to modify the CDM-hypothesis, I submit such claims are premature: the simulations contain too many idealizations and are too ill-understood to draw any final conclusions about ΛCDM (De Baerdemaeker & Boyd, 2020). The only conclusion that can be drawn at this point is that making progress on the dark matter problem will require an iterative exchange between searches for dark matter candidates, cosmological and astrophysical observations, and complex modeling efforts.

3.4 Realism about Dark Matter

Dark matter also raises new challenges for the metaphysics of science. As has become clear so far, dark matter is an extension of or complement to scientific theories with a long-standing history. In some ways, it falls outside of the scope of established physics. Worse, because it doesn't interact electromagnetically, we can't 'see' dark matter structures (Jacquart, 2020; Weisberg et al., 2018) in the way that other astronomical objects are seen. What does all this imply for the scientific realist? (For the scientific anti-realist, dark sector physics doesn't seem different from other unobservables). Recall from Section 2.3 that scientific realism is committed to the existence of both observables and unobservables that are posited by our best scientific theories. If one is a scientific realist, should one be committed to the existence of dark matter?

As was mentioned before, contemporary views on scientific realism are selective in various ways. They don't imply commitment to the existence of *any* entity or structure postulated by our current best scientific theories. The key question is: does dark matter clear the threshold for realist commitment? In the limited philosophical literature on dark matter realism, the early consensus seemed to fall on anti-realism (Allzén, 2021; Martens, 2022) (although see Dellsén 2019, for an opposing view).

Martens provides the most detailed argument, building on Chakravartty's (2017) breakdown of realism into three different commitments: metaphysical, semantic, and epistemic. The metaphysical commitment is to a mind-independent reality. The semantic commitment is that scientific claims have truth-value. The epistemic commitment is that scientific claims are actually true.

Martens takes issue with the semantic commitment when it comes to dark matter. Following De Baerdemaeker (2021) and Martens (2022), let us refer to everything that is currently broadly accepted about dark matter based on cosmology and astrophysics as the 'common core' dark matter concept: this is the core of properties that all dark matter candidates have to satisfy to qualify as dark matter. This includes that dark matter is nonbaryonic, electromagnetically neutral, slow-moving, and that it constitutes 27% of the current energy density of the universe.

Martens argues that this common core concept of dark matter is too thin to warrant realism:

> The problem with dark matter realism is not a lack of viable suggestions, i.e. models, concerning the nature of dark matter, but rather their abundance – or, more precisely, the thin common conceptual core of this cornucopia. (Martens, 2022, 3)

The issue, it seems, is that because this common core still permits so many dark matter candidates with such widely varying properties (one would be hard-pressed to call primordial black holes and axions similar), this core is too vague to warrant any semantic realist commitment. Simply put, we wouldn't know what we are realists about if we were to adopt a realist stance to dark matter.

Instead, Martens adheres to an "indefinitely suspended realism" (7) about dark matter. This leaves the door open for future realism about dark matter. If future scientific work would make the dark matter concept more precise and limit the underdetermination of models, then "semantic and epistemological realism would be vindicated simultaneously" (9). For instance, if dark matter searches turn out to be successful, or astrophysical and cosmological work puts tighter constraints on the space of possibilities, realism would be back on the table. Importantly, even if full-fledged dark matter realism is warranted in the future, that would still not imply that we would have been warranted to be dark matter realists today.

Vaynberg (2024) has recently provided a response to Martens. Vaynberg begins by arguing that the thin common core dark matter concept that emerges out of cosmology and astrophysics, while minimal, is the concept "in virtue of which [dark matter] is causally connected to the phenomena it is supposed to explain" (6). That means that the concept is kind-constitutive. Furthermore, Vaynberg argues that there is empirical evidence supporting the existence of dark matter as defined by this thin common-core concept, thanks to the observations of the Bullet Cluster.

I agree with Vaynberg. While I concur with Martens that the current dark matter concept is fairly thin and that there are a large number of models that are still compatible with that thin common core, it is also the case that there are plenty of models that are *not* compatible with it, like neutrinos or massive compact halo objects. This, to me, provides grounds for a modest semantic realist commitment: scientific theories including dark matter posit the existence of something that is compatible with that common core. This 'something' plays an important explanatory role in cosmology and astrophysics. To be sure, what I am suggesting is a realist commitment to a vague concept. But that doesn't seem to be a *prima facie* problem.

4 Dark Energy

While dark matter makes up little over a quarter of the current energy density of the universe, the bulk of the dark sector is dark energy. Like dark matter, dark energy is so far only detected through its gravitational effects. Unlike dark matter, there is only one such effect: the accelerated expansion of the universe. This 1998 discovery was awarded the 2011 Nobel Prize in Physics, with good reason. In a universe with only gravitating matter content, the expansion of the universe was expected to slow down over time due to gravitational pull. Sandage famously described cosmology as 'the search for two numbers': the Hubble parameter and the deceleration parameter. An accelerated expansion implied that the energy density of the universe required a different makeup; it suggested a new type of contribution with a different equation of state. This became dark energy, represented by the cosmological constant Λ.

Or at least, so the story goes. In practice, the discovery and acceptance of the accelerated expansion of the universe came after a long history of grappling with Λ (Section 4.1). And with the acceptance of the accelerated expansion and a nonzero cosmological constant, an old acquaintance came front and center again: the cosmological constant problem (Section 4.2).[18]

---

[18] The reintroduction of Λ also led to a revival of de Sitter spacetime in cosmology. I refer readers interested in the philosophical implications of the de Sitter renaissance to Belot (2023).

4.1 The History of the Cosmological Constant

As "Λ: the constant that refuses to die", the title of Earman's (2001) review of the history of the cosmological constant suggests, Λ has never fully disappeared from relativistic cosmology since it first appeared in 1917. Einstein (1917) introduced a nonzero cosmological constant in a model of a closed and static universe, primarily motivated by matters of philosophical taste: Einstein sought to model a homogeneous static universe (assumed to be the case for the actual universe), while also satisfying Mach's principle and the relativity principle (Earman, 2001, 192-193). By 1931, the former point had already become moot. The cosmology community broadly accepted the expansion of the universe based on Hubble's observational results (Hubble, 1929; Hubble & Humason, 1931) and theoretical work by Friedman (1999/1922) and Lemaître (1927). Note that this did not immediately lead to the rejection of the cosmological constant: the Eddington-Lemaître cosmological model, which was the consensus view for a brief time around 1931, modeled a closed, uniformly expanding universe starting from an (unstable) Einstein universe extending to $t = -\infty$, with a nonzero cosmological constant (De Baerdemaeker & Schneider, 2022).

The first model of an expanding universe with $\Lambda = 0$ was published by Einstein in 1931, but it gained little attention (O'Raifeartaigh et al., 2014). Einstein and de Sitter published an even simpler model in 1932: theirs was a monotonically expanding universe from an initial singularity. Despite these theoretical developments, and although Einstein had started to express unease with Λ relatively soon after first introducing it in 1917 (Earman, 2001; O'Raifeartaigh & Mitton, 2018), Λ stuck around long after the 1930s. There were several reasons for this.

First, the aforementioned cosmological models were not very well-known nor in line with other ideas about the universe. Einstein's 1931 model went unnoticed for a long time. And at least according to Eddington (1938, 128), neither Einstein nor de Sitter considered their expanding universe model from 1932 particularly interesting. Einstein and de Sitter's model was also the first explicitly open-universe model, while the preference for a closed universe seemed to have permeated cosmology for several decades (de Swart, 2020).[19] Second, from a theoretical perspective, introducing the cosmological constant

---

[19] As an aside, I believe that the question of when the universe 'opened up' is, as of today, still unanswered. Many seem to assume that the Einstein-de Sitter model from 1932 is that time, but this is clearly too simple. Mike D. Schneider and I have a working hypothesis that it is more likely this opening up took place between the late 1960s (with Hawking, Penrose, and Geroch's work on black holes) and the 1980s (with the development of inflation). Note that in the 1970s, there was still a preference for a closed universe, which, as de Swart et al. (2017) argue, was one of the theoretical motivations behind the dark matter hypothesis.

is a natural part of general relativity. Including the cosmological constant term gives the most general version of the Einstein Field Equations, with Λ an undetermined constant. This was already pointed out to Einstein by Tolman, who argued that this implied that the value of Λ could not be decided arbitrarily (Earman, 2001, 197). Instead, Tolman advocated for it being determined empirically (the other alternative being to provide strong theoretical arguments for a particular value). Third, and in line with Tolman's concerns, there was a serious empirical reason in the 1930s to set $\Lambda \neq 0$: the timescale problem. Based on Hubble's velocity-distance relation, the age of the universe based on its expansion history was thought to be an order of magnitude younger than the age of the oldest stars, thus also not permitting sufficient time for structure formation. This was the main motivation for Lemaître, for example, to hold on to a nonzero cosmological constant. It allowed him to introduce a 'coasting phase' in the expansion of the universe, such that the universe was older than the second expansion phase (De Baerdemaeker & Schneider, 2022). And finally, some, like Eddington, had theoretical preferences for a nonzero cosmological constant (Earman, 2001, 203).

Some of these concerns disappeared in the second half of the twentieth century. Eddington's theoretical musings were not successful, and the Einstein-de Sitter model gained prominence as the standard model of cosmology (see for instance Weinberg's (1972) seminal textbook). Meanwhile, thanks to Sandage's (1958) and Baade's (1956) work correcting Hubble's distance measurements, the original timescale problem disappeared. That meant that the available empirical observations could be modeled with $\Lambda = 0$.

Again, however, this didn't mean that Λ disappeared from view (Earman, 2001, §10). Tolman's argument still stood: Λ is part of the generalized Einstein Field Equations, with an undetermined – albeit bounded by observations – value. The search for a theoretical argument for the cosmological constant's value was on. Beginning with Zel'dovich in the 1960s, particle physicists started to show interest in cosmology, and particularly in the cosmological constant. The realization dawned that the energy density of the vacuum behaves like a cosmological constant and that it should therefore be possible to derive a prediction for its value based on quantum field theoretic (QFT) considerations (Earman, 2001, 207).

However, it quickly became clear that the value derived for Λ from QFT was orders of magnitude too large compared to the empirically determined upper bound – so large that the expansion of the universe would have happened too rapidly to allow for structure formation, let alone the development of human life. To solve this issue, one could assume that the vacuum energy density contributes to the effective cosmological constant Λ_{eff} together with a 'bare' cosmological constant Λ_0:

$$\Lambda_{\it eff} = \Lambda_0 + 8\pi G \langle \rho_{vac} \rangle \tag{6}$$

Λ_0 is a free parameter that can cancel out the vacuum energy density contribution ρ_{vac}. This solution is hardly satisfactory, however: the value of Λ_0 would have to be fine-tuned to cancel out over 118 decimal places to keep $\Lambda_{\it eff}$ in line with observational bounds. Weinberg (1989, 1) proclaimed this problem "one veritable crisis": the cosmological constant problem (CCP). The CCP motivated decades of searches for some 'natural' solution to the problem, where an unknown type of symmetry would justify setting $\Lambda_{\it eff}$ to zero despite the large zero-point energies predicted by QFT (Koberinski, Falck, and Smeenk, 2023).

In the 1990s, cracks started to appear in the case for naturalness due to new empirical anomalies. Starting in the 1980s, a new timescale problem emerged, this time related to globular star clusters. These are tightly gravitationally bound clusters of stars, often found in the halo of spiral galaxies like the Milky Way. Astrophysicists generally assume that stars in such clusters all formed around the same time, so they all have approximately the same age. Weinberg (1989, 8) mentioned that the estimated globular cluster age was older than the estimated expansion age of the universe, leading some to propose non-zero values for Λ. The age estimates for globular clusters were not sufficient to force a general acceptance of $\Lambda \neq 0$, however. That would require stronger, less model-dependent empirical evidence.

In 1998, this evidence was put forward by two competing teams working on supernova cosmology: the Supernova Cosmology Project and the High-z Collaboration. Supernova cosmology uses the fact that Type Ia supernovae (SNe Ia) are highly uniform to probe the evolution of the universe. SNe Ia that are observed at higher redshift reveal the deeper past of the universe. Guralp (2020) gives a detailed historical reconstruction of the preambles and studies that ultimately led to the discovery of the accelerating expansion of the universe. The rest of this subsection is based on Guralp's account.

While supernova cosmology had its start in the 1980s, it didn't get properly going until the 1990s.[20] One of the main hurdles was to find sufficient SNe Ia to achieve meaningful results. After revising their search method, the Supernova Cosmology Project published their first measurement for cosmological parameters in 1997. The results were wrong: they measured $\Lambda = 0$ matter density parameter $\Omega_M \approx 1$ (Guralp, 2020, §3.2-3.3). The High-z Collaboration went through a similar prehistory (Guralp, 2020, §3.4). However, despite these erroneous results, Guralp shows that the early papers were essential in

---

[20] On the earlier history of establishing the distance ladder, including the usefulness of supernovae, see Holmes (2024).

establishing the reliability of supernova cosmology and the teams' respective methodologies.

By 1998, both teams were prepared to unleash the full potential of their newly established measurement protocols. In the span of less than a year, the two teams announced their surprising results that the universe's expansion was not slowing down but speeding up, and that $\Lambda > 0$.

Given the aforementioned history of the cosmological constant and especially the expected naturalness arguments for $\Lambda = 0$, the evidence claims by the two teams needed to be extraordinarily strong. Guralp identifies two ways in which robustness arguments helped strengthen the evidence.[21] First, each team internally ran several types of data analyses (The Supernova Cosmology Project used different subsets of the data; the High-z Collaboration, which had less supernovae in its data set, used different analysis techniques) (Guralp, 2020, §3.5-3.6). Second, the fact that two competing teams announced the same result around the same time, helped convince the broader community of its accuracy (Guralp, 2020, §4). In an oral interview conducted by Guralp, Riess (High-z) recalled:

> Now look at it from a community standpoint. They hear this crazy result but they see two different teams which they knew were not collaborative, they were competitive. Yet they were getting this same result. [...] They say "well I guess this must be the right answer because both teams get it". Scientists love to cross-check. (Guralp, 2020, 37)

In other words, there was a strong robustness argument on the table.

In subsequent years, more and (according to Guralp) different robustness arguments became available through consistency checks with the CMB power spectrum. The WMAP results showed the universe being close to flat, but the matter contributions to the energy density only amounting to approximately 0.3 of the critical density (Spergel et al., 2003). The remaining 0.7 can be contributed by a nonzero cosmological constant, or, in other words, dark energy. (The term dark energy was coined by Turner after the publication of the supernovae results as an umbrella term for whatever causes the accelerated expansion of the universe.) Thus, the cosmological constant came back from the dead, and stronger than ever.

4.2 The Cosmological Constant Problem(s)

The reintroduction of a nonzero cosmological constant brought back the CCP in a new guise. When Weinberg first introduced the CCP as a crisis, Λ was still an

---

[21] Robustness arguments were also discussed in context of dark matter searches (Section 3.3).

undetermined constant, albeit bounded by the fact that any form of life is possible[22] and with all observations consistent with it being effectively zero. And while the discrepancy with the zero-point energy density was an issue, there was, at least at the time, hope for a solution via a naturalness argument. All in all, the only challenge was the so-called 'old CCP': explaining the discrepancy between $\langle \rho_{vac} \rangle$ being large and Λ zero.

The supernovae results gave an exact empirical determination of Λ for the first time. The conflict with the zero-point energy remained an issue (the observed value of Λ is still many orders of magnitude smaller than any prediction for zero-point energy), but it added the difficulty that a solution through naturalness became implausible. This is what philosophers of science often refer to as the 'new CCP': the discrepancy between $\langle \rho_{vac} \rangle$ being large and Λ being small-but-not-zero. While a solution to Weinberg's original problem may have seemed within reach, the new CCP seems more of a veritable crisis because it lacks an obvious route to a solution.

The supernovae results also raised a new question: what is the physics behind the cosmological constant? In other words, what drives the accelerated expansion of the universe? If not vacuum energy density, then what? Following a recent review (Foundational Aspects of Dark Energy (FADE) Collaboration et al., 2023) I will refer to this as the 'dark energy problem'.[23]

The status of the CCP, old or new, as a problem has been philosophically contentious. Denoting the CCP as a genuine problem or 'crisis' means that the CCP is a persisting anomaly for current theory. Philosophical debates center around whether the CCP really is a problem, what the CCP is a problem for, and what permissible solutions to the CCP look like (Earman, 2001; Koberinski, 2021; Schneider, 2020). Here, I'll primarily focus on the new CCP, although the dark energy problem will make an appearance as well.

There are several reasons why philosophers of science have been critical of framing the CCP as a crisis. For one, some take issue with the assumptions required for setting up the CCP in the first place. Koberinski (2021) identifies three problematic steps in setting up the CCP as a conflict between the

---

[22] Koberinski et al. (2023) identify this as a form of 'weak anthropic reasoning'.
[23] Foundational Aspects of Dark Energy (FADE) Collaboration et al. (2023) actually identifies four distinct challenges related to the cosmological constant. First, the new CCP as discussed earlier – which they refer to as the 'old CCP'. Second, the question of what fuels the accelerated expansion of the universe – in other words, what is 'dark energy'? This is the 'dark energy problem'. Third, the 'classical CCP' is about phase transitions affecting potential energy contributions to the vacuum energies. Finally, what they refer to as the 'new CCP' is the UV-sensitivity of the vacuum energy. While especially the latter will be relevant to the discussion the discussion that follows, I refrain from adopting their terminology because it conflicts with philosophical habit.

calculated value of the vacuum energy density from QFT on the one hand, and the observed value for the cosmological constant on the other. First, Koberinski sheds doubt on the fact that there even *is* such an absolute value for $\langle \rho_{vac} \rangle$, given that the true vacuum term never appears in quantum field theoretic calculations. Second, Koberinski argues that the calculation of $\langle \rho_{vac} \rangle$ is problematic, because it is a divergent term. That means that to calculate $\langle \rho_{vac} \rangle$, a cutoff energy scale needs to be introduced, and although *any* reasonable cutoff leads to a conflicting measurement with Λ_{obs}, there are no grounds to assume that the divergences of $\langle \rho_{vac} \rangle$ will be cured at higher energy scales. Koberinski is hesitant to trust a divergent term in QFT for which no mechanism for its regularization exists. Third, Koberinski questions how the vacuum energy density couples to gravity. As a result, Koberinski concludes that the CCP should not be taken seriously. Indeed, even though the CCP "has undoubtedly been successful as a heuristic motivator [...], no clear solution strategy has led to major progress in developing quantum gravity" (Koberinski, 2021, 276). Koberinski and Smeenk (2023) further argue that the CCP only arises if one assumes that effective field theoretic methods should apply for understanding Λ.

Even if one buys into the technical setup of the problem, there is a further reason why some have argued that the CCP does not amount to a crisis – at least not for current theory. Schneider (2020) points out that setting up the CCP requires an additional assumption: that the observed value for the cosmological constant Λ_{eff} is exhausted by the zero-point energies arising in QFT. However, as is already clear from Equation (6), there is no reason why one would not be permitted to introduce a bare cosmological constant term Λ_0 to cancel out the contributions. There are different ways of interpreting this bare term, but as it stands, "its function in the [cosmological] model is that of a fit parameter to help match the model to empirical data" (Schneider, 2020, 5).

The issue with this solution is that the calculated value for $\langle \rho_{vac} \rangle$ depends on the energy cutoff scale (Wallace, 2021). That means that Λ_0 becomes a function *both* of the observed cosmological constant, and the arbitrarily chosen high-energy cutoff scale. Moreover, as Koberinski acknowledges, $\langle \rho_{vac} \rangle$ will be many orders of magnitude larger than the observed value even for very low cutoff scales. Λ_0 would therefore need to be fine-tuned to an extraordinarily high degree regardless of the cutoff scale, but differently for each cutoff scale. Wallace (2021, fn.35) points out that "the relationships between bare and observed parameters in particle physics are *not* generally fine-tuned in this way". So even if there is no strict empirical anomaly for current theory, the CCP does make for an unusual case of fine-tuning.

Of course, as was discussed in context of inflation (Section 2.1), establishing that fine-tuning is problematic is a notoriously hard philosophical problem, and

Wallace (2021, 34) concedes that one can debate whether fine-tuning to this degree is a problem at all (Wallace clearly sees it as such). At the very least, though, Wallace is right that the fact that Λ_0 as a fit parameter is dependent on an arbitrary calculational choice signals a gap in current theory.

When it comes to the technical setup of the problem, Wallace takes a stronger stance. Wallace points out that the CCP arises out of fairly straightforward calculations in so-called 'Low-Energy Quantum Gravity' (LEQG), that is, "the theory one obtains by treating GR as an effective field theory, quantized through path-integral means" (Wallace, 2021, 36). LEQG is behind a lot of contemporary cosmology and astrophysics, and as such has proven to be highly successful. Wallace considers this success of LEQG important for two reasons. First, it gives a strong rebuttal against the technical concerns about the setup of the CCP. Second, the success of LEQG helps explain why the CCP is a central problem in contemporary physics: it is one of the few pointers that physicists currently have to a successor theory for LEQG, that is, to a more complete theory of quantum gravity.

Although Schneider (2020), unlike Wallace, is not willing to take fine-tuning as sufficient to establish the CCP as a problem for current theory, Schneider does agree with Wallace on its importance as a pointer for future theory. After all, rejecting the CCP as a genuine problem raises a puzzle: if the CCP is *not* a problem for current theory, why is it so widely discussed by scientists?

Schneider suggests that the CCP serves as a motivation for future theorizing (see also Schneider 2022). Specifically, different assumptions about what a future theory of quantum gravity will look like motivate different formulations of the CCP. Each formulation then fits as a 'problem-that-is-already-solved' by the relevant preferred future theory of quantum gravity. Schneider identifies three different categories of solutions, related to three different assumptions about quantum gravity and three different versions of the CCP:

1. Assume that vacuum quantities [...] do not gravitate as ordinary sources in the EFE. Then the CCP becomes: What gives rise to the effective vacuum term characterized by Λ in the standard model of cosmology?
2. Assume that zero-point energies gravitate as tensorial quantities on the right-hand side of the EFE and exhaustively source the effective vacuum term characterized by Λ. Then the CCP becomes: How does one account for the discrepancy between the currently computed values of the zero-point energies and the observed Λ?
3. Assume that Λ is not exhaustively sourced by vacuum energies. Then the CCP becomes: What other physical mechanisms can contribute to that which is now understood as the effective vacuum termed characterized by Λ?

(Schneider, 2020, 11)

Note that all three types of solutions don't just solve the new CCP, they also solve the dark energy problem. That is, they give a causal explanation for the accelerated expansion of the universe, either by introducing new types of matter fields, or by modifying general relativity.

This is not obviously the case for two other types of solutions to the new CCP. The first alternative solution is just assuming that Λ is a free parameter for which the value can be determined by observations. That value should be accepted as a brute fact. There are two issues with this attitude. First, it completely ignores the CCP, which at least according to Wallace (2021) is not a tenable epistemic attitude. Second, from the perspective of practicing scientists, this attitude closes off any possibility for further inquiry (Koberinski et al., 2023; Schneider, 2020; Wallace, 2021). And since pointers for a more complete theory of quantum gravity are slim, we better make use of the few that are available.

The other type of solution that doesn't explicitly address the dark energy problem is anthropic solutions to the CCP. This type of solution aims to give some probabilistic argument as to why the observed value of Λ is to be expected, on the assumption that we live in a multiverse (due to eternal inflation or string theory, for instance). In other words, the observed value of Λ is explained statistically, rather than dynamically. There are various issues with anthropic solutions. Similar to the measure problem in inflation, Benétreau-Dupin (2015) has argued that there are serious issues with the probabilistic arguments. Perhaps more concerning, anthropic solutions still suffer from UV-sensitivity: the landscape of possibilities out of which the observed value of Λ is selected depends on the chosen energy scale. Finally, Koberinski et al. (2023, 25) point out that these solutions inevitably rely on speculative physics generating a multiverse. Without separate reasons to trust the speculative physics suggesting the multiverse, it seems premature to accept this type of solution to the CCP and to close off further inquiry into other routes.

To end this section, let me briefly note that there is an alternative way to make progress on the dark energy problem at least: observational programs. Currently, several experiments are underway to either constrain the equation of state of dark energy (the hope is that this equation of state will prove to be time-dependent) or to find evidence of modified theories of gravity on cosmological scales (effects which would have to be minute, given the strong constraints on modified gravity from solar-system tests of GR). Ideally, these observations will shed light on the physics behind Λ and break the serious underdetermination between the many theoretical proposals (Koberinski et al., 2023; Smeenk & Weatherall, 2023). Some are skeptical that such cosmological observations can be sufficient to break the underdetermination between

Philosophy of Cosmology and Astrophysics 39

different proposals for the microphysical mechanism responsible for the accelerated expansion of the universe. Instead, they are concerned that cosmology may be stuck in a state of permanent underdetermination on this subject (Ferreira, Wolf, and Read, 2025; Wolf & Ferreira, 2023). Suffice to say: to be continued.

5 Black Holes

The final case I want to focus on is black hole astrophysics. Black hole research is about as old as general relativity: Schwarzschild found his eponymous solution to the Einstein field equations already in 1916. But for a long while, the physical reality of singularities remained controversial and it received limited attention in physics (Earman, 1995, Ch. 1). In the 1960s, there was a true renaissance of theoretical black hole research. The singularity theorems of Hawking, Penrose and others demonstrated the generic nature of spacetime singularities, and Hawking's first theoretical argument for the existence of Hawking radiation laid the foundations for black hole thermodynamics (see Earman 1995, for references and a philosophical introduction).

Observational results for stellar-mass black holes followed fairly quickly. Also in the 1960s, Cygnus X-1, a bright galactic source of X-rays was discovered. Further studies revealed that Cygnus X-1 was a binary for which one of the companions was inferred to be a black hole due to its high mass density (see Avni & Bahcall 1975, for one of the early studies of Cygnus X-1's mass; various recent studies have updated the mass estimates). Empirical evidence for supermassive black holes took much longer. Only in the early 2000s did scientists find convincing empirical evidence that Sagittarius A* (Sgr A*), the massive object at the center of the Milky Way, is a supermassive black hole (Genzel et al., 1997; Ghez et al., 1998; Ghez et al., 2000). Long-term X-ray observations showed stars rapidly orbiting a central mass which, due to the high rotational velocities of the stars and the small radius of the central mass, couldn't be anything but a black hole. Curiel (2019, 28) submits it is only at this stage that "the community achieved something like unanimous agreement on the existence and relevance of black holes".

Today, black hole research is at the center of many more disciplines than cosmology and astrophysics: research ranges from quantum gravity to foundations of (semi-)classical relativity and beyond. This section will only touch on black hole astrophysics. Readers interested in other philosophical aspects of black holes, including the information loss paradox, the validity of black hole thermodynamics, and the implications of the existence of singularities for the metaphysics of spacetime could look at (Curiel, 2019; Dougherty & Callender, 2016; Earman, 1995) and references therein as a starting point; those interested in getting a sense of the wildly different types of research that black holes inspire would also enjoy Gallison's documentary "Black Holes: The Edge of All we Know",[24] where philosophers, astrophysicists, theoretical physicists, and experimental physicists all discuss their respective black hole research.

As an example of astrophysical research, black hole astrophysics is both an exception to and an exemplar of typical observational astrophysics. It is an exception because black holes do not emit detectable electromagnetic radiation, unlike most stars and galaxies. In that sense, it is similar to astrophysical dark matter research. Moreover, they generally evolve on much shorter timescales than most astrophysical objects, whose typical timescales tend to be of the order of millions of years (Doboszewski & Lehmkuhl, 2023). One exception to this rule is the formation timeline for binary systems including a black hole (Elder, 2023b).

Black hole astrophysics is an exemplar of the multifaceted nature of observational astrophysics. Observational astrophysicists in general do not restrict themselves to passively detecting electromagnetic signals; they also experiment on analogue systems, search for different kinds of signals (it was a black hole merger that ushered in a new era of multi-messenger astronomy), and conduct complex modeling. This section's discussion of black hole astrophysics is the final stepping-stone for a general discussion of how scientists gain empirical access to the universe.[25]

5.1 What Is a Black Hole?

Before discussing black hole astrophysics specifically, I want to take a step back and reflect on the broad range of disciplines that study black holes. Since there are so many disciplines, there are many different ways of defining black holes. Based on an informal survey of physicists and philosophers from various sub-fields, Curiel (2019) identifies at least twelve working definitions which are not necessarily mutually compatible. While reviewing some of the common definitions (e.g., the classical event horizon, a singularity), Curiel also highlights that each of these definitions has shortcomings. For instance, astrophysicists in practice define a black hole as "a system of at least a minimum mass, spatially small enough that relativistic effects cannot be ignored" (Curiel, 2019, 30). But, as Curiel points out, this definition could also be satisfied by a

---

[24] https://www.blackholefilm.com/.
[25] That being said, it is noteworthy that the philosophical literature on astrophysics so far has tended to focus on more peculiar cases in astrophysics, like black holes and dark matter. Much less attention has been paid to the 'bread and butter' research on more typical stars and galaxies. I will return to this point in the conclusion.

naked singularity, which are supposedly forbidden by Penrose's cosmic censorship conjecture. For each of the proposed definitions, Curiel identifies similar pitfalls, reasons why they cannot be 'the' universal definition of a black hole.

This raises an obvious challenge. These definitions, despite not being equivalent and sometimes even being incompatible, "are all at bottom trying to get at the same thing" (Curiel, 2019, 32). In other words, the astrophysicists of the Event Horizon Telescope, the condensed matter physicists studying analogue black holes (more on both later), the theoretical physicists studying semi-classical gravity, they all purport to study the same class of objects. Without an agreed upon definition – indeed, without an agreed upon common core similar to the thin definition of dark matter (Section 3.3), it's hard to see how the case can be made that all of these definitions are studying the same 'thing'. But, as Curiel stresses, making this case is essential for applying results from one area of black hole research to another (32).

What is to be done in response to this conundrum? Doboszewski and Lehmkuhl (2023) identify six possible responses. Curiel's take, they argue, aligns with pragmatic pluralism. Curiel considers "black hole":

> a rough, nebulous concept [...] shared across physics, that one can explicate [...] by articulating a more or less precise definition that captures in a clear way many important features of the nebulous idea, [which] can be done in many different ways, each appropriate for different theoretical, observational, and foundational contexts. (Curiel, 2019, 33)

In other words, the fact that there are many different ways to make the nebulous concept of a black hole more precise is seen as a good thing, because this flexibility permits scientists from so many different sub-disciplines to adapt the concept to their specific research questions. Of course, on this take, it is not clear how Curiel expects it to be possible to apply results across research fields.

Doboszewski and Lehmkuhl (2023) have a different view. They review the relationships between some definitions and point out that these relationships "typically flow from the empirical and conceptual adequacy of an exact solution of Einstein's field equations, in particular the Kerr and Schwarzschild solutions" (240). Given this commonality, it seems plausible that these exact solutions are the common core concept of a black hole. Whence then the plurality of definitions that Curiel's survey revealed? That, they argue, is due to the introduction of various auxiliary assumptions that are required by the specific research context in which the common core concept is to be applied. In other words, the common core definition, that is, the exact solution to the Einstein field equations, is a highly idealized concept that needs to be de-idealized in various ways depending on the specific purpose.

While I am sympathetic to this position, there remains a lingering question. What does all of this imply for the metaphysics of black holes (also discussed by Allzén 2023)? If the common core concept of a black hole is known to be a highly idealized concept that does not actually apply anywhere in nature (this is part of the concern Curiel raises about the classical definitions), and it is not clear how each practical definition relates to the common core, what then, can the realist commitment latch on to? More work is required to clarify this point.

5.2 'Direct' Detection of a Black Hole

Even within the sub-discipline of black hole astrophysics, several epistemic puzzles appear. In the last decade, two milestones were reached in black hole astrophysics: the first detection of gravitational waves by the LIGO/Virgo consortium, and the first image of the event horizon and its immediate surroundings by the Event Horizon Telescope (EHT) collaboration. Interestingly enough, both collaborations explicitly or implicitly made claims of 'directness': LIGO/Virgo claimed the first "direct" detection of gravitational waves and the first "direct" observation of a binary black hole merger (Abbott et al., 2016), while the EHT touted its image of Sgr A* (the second image they released) as the "first direct visual evidence" that Sgr A* is a supermassive black hole (Event Horizon Telescope, 2022).[26]

A historical study by Skulberg and Elder (forthcoming) shows that language of "directness" in black hole imaging has a storied history. Still, this type of language is surprising to encounter in context of black hole research. Black holes, much like dark matter, are generically described as unobservable. Black holes are perfect absorbers (Hawking radiation would not be observable to a human observer – more on this in the next subsection). Black holes also have an event horizon, that is, they are a region of no escape. For an external observer, it is impossible to observe what happens inside the event horizon. Eckart et al. (2017, 555) therefore describe (supermassive[27]) black holes as "unobservable entities" or "only observable by indirect means". They further claim that we can only ever infer their existence based on their interactions with their surroundings, for example, their effects on a binary companion, an accretion disk, or through gravitational lensing effects.

---

[26] Note that while it may be tempting to draw parallels with the jargon of "direct" and "indirect" dark matter experiments, that would be inappropriate. The language surrounding dark matter experiments is signaling different types of experimental probes, but it is not clear to me that this language is meant to signal epistemic implications. In the context of gravitational wave detections, it is more plausible that scientists wanted to make an epistemic distinction.

[27] Although Eckart et al. (2017) focus solely on supermassive black holes, the reasons for them being not directly observable apply to all types of black holes.

There seems to be a tension in the description of the recent breakthrough results in observational black hole astrophysics, and the scientific reality that black holes are not in any intuitive sense directly observable. Elder (2020, 2023a, 2023b, 2025) has taken on the task of clarifying the epistemology of gravitational wave astrophysics, including the use of 'direct' or 'indirect' in describing various observational results in black hole astrophysics. As Elder stresses, these terms are socially and politically laden, but there are also certain epistemic implications that may follow from them.

Elder (2025) focuses on the LIGO/Virgo-results, which claimed the first "direct detection" of gravitational waves, and the first "direct observation" of a binary black hole merger (see Collins 2017, for a detailed history of this result). When it comes to the gravitational-wave detection, the directness qualification was meant to distinguish the new results from the 1970s observations of the Hulse-Taylor pulsar, a binary star system. Those observations revealed orbital decay in the pulsar: the distance between the two companions had decreased over time due to a loss of energy in the system. The energy loss corresponded exactly to the expected energy loss due to gravitational waves. This is widely considered to be convincing evidence for the existence of gravitational waves. In contrast, the LIGO/Virgo consortium detected gravitational waves for the first time in a terrestrial detector: the gravitational waves caused a slight disturbance in two perpendicular laser beams being reflected off hanging mirrors. For their first detection (as well as most subsequent ones), the signal was identified through matching it with an expected wave form for gravitational waves. Based on the detected signal, it was then inferred that the gravitational waves were due to a binary black hole merger.[28]

Building on work from Hacking, Shapere, Franklin, and Parker, Elder (2025) argues that the LIGO/Virgo collaboration's directness claim was justified in the case of gravitational wave detection, thus setting it apart from the Hulse-Taylor pulsar. Elder first points out that both the LIGO/Virgo detection and the Hulse-Taylor pulsar observations require complex detectors (interferometers or telescopes) and various modeling assumptions. Thus, both of their detections are in fact inferences from raw data (instrument readings) to the phenomenon of gravitational waves. However, the LIGO/Virgo detection was direct because:

> the LIGO interferometers are gravitational wave detectors. The "raw instrument reading" is strain data, representing a feature of the entity being measured – the strain associated with a passing gravitational wave. In modeling this system, the interferometer can essentially be black boxed as a mapping from the target system to a selective representation of that system. (9)

---

[28] The explanation in this paragraph sells the complexity of gravitational wave detection hopelessly short. Elder (2020) gives an extensive and accessible summary.

The reason why the interferometer can be black-boxed in the inference from the raw data to a gravitational-wave signal, is that the interferometer has been adequately calibrated and tested as a gravitational-wave detector. Contrast this with the Hulse-Taylor pulsar observations, which Elder classifies as indirect. There, the instruments that scientists could intervene on to calibrate and test was the radio telescope. The instrument was a detector of electromagnetic waves, not gravitational waves. The inference to gravitational waves required a further layer of inference about a separate target system (the pulsar). This layer of inference could not be black-boxed based on pre-existing knowledge of the detector (10). Importantly, Elder does not want to attach any general evaluation to directness or indirectness: both types can be epistemically powerful or suspect. Rather, the distinction indicates that there are different challenges to overcome in securing the reliability of the detection depending on whether it is direct or indirect (10).

Elder further evaluates whether the claim of a 'direct observation' of a binary black hole merger by the LIGO/Virgo collaboration was justified, and concludes that it was not. The inference to the binary black hole merger was based on a model of *both* the gravitational wave detector and the detected gravitational wave signal (Elder, 2025, 10). As such, it was more similar to the Hulse-Taylor pulsar observations as evidence for gravitational waves, than the LIGO/Virgo-detections.

Elder's analysis of (in)directness can also be applied to the evidence for Sgr A* being a supermassive black hole. Recall that the first strong evidence consisted of long-term observations of stars orbiting the object in the galactic center. Their orbital speed was so high, that the object needed to be extremely massive. The inference to the presence of a supermassive black hole required both modeling the telescope used for observations, as well as the orbiting stars. Skulberg and Elder (forthcoming) conclude that this qualifies as an indirect inference on Elder's account.

This indirectness also seems to be at the root of some philosophical discussion as to the strength of the evidence for Sgr A* being a supermassive black hole prior to the EHT results. Given its intrinsic unobservability, Eckart et al. (2017) raise an underdetermination worry: while a supermassive black hole is one possible explanation for the motion of the orbiting stars, there are some alternative explanations like GRAVASTARS or boson stars. In other words, the models were not specific enough to empirically rule out alternatives. Doboszewski and Lehmkuhl (2023, 233-234) argue that the inference to a supermassive black hole takes the form of an inference to the best explanation.

This reconstruction does not remove the underdetermination – in their view, this would require probing the spacetime geometry right outside of a black hole – but it helps understanding the nature of the underdetermination.

The underdetermination is not pernicious. Even without conclusive evidence to eliminate alternatives, there are several reasons to not be *too* concerned about the underdetermination of the nature of Sgr A*. First, as Eckart et al. (2017) themselves argue, many of the alternative explanations suffer severe theoretical challenges, including the fact that some likely would have collapsed into a black hole during the formation or accretion phase. Second, the EHT has provided new empirical evidence for Sgr A*: it has significantly tightened the size estimates for the horizon to the order of the Schwarzschild radius. This also explains why the EHT press release announcing the Sgr A* results touts the observations as the "first direct visual evidence" that Sgr A* is a supermassive black hole (Event Horizon Telescope, 2022).

Finally, how do the EHT imaging efforts play out as far as Elder's account of direct or indirect observation goes? The EHT uses a technique called 'very long baseline interferometry' (VLBI). The basic concept is the following: telescopes positioned around the earth simultaneously observe the same object, Sgr A*, several days in a row. This generates enormous amounts of data. By cleverly combining the images from the different telescopes together, scientists are able to 'fill in the gaps' between the different telescopes. As a result, they in practice have created a telescope that is the size of the entire Earth – a size that is essential to be able to observe an object as far away and as compact as Sgr A*.[29]

Elder (2025, 10-11) (see also Skulberg and Elder, forthcoming) recognizes that this case is difficult to assess. On the one hand, the raw data is about visibilities, not about a black hole. To get to the image of the black hole published by the EHT collaboration, complex imaging algorithms were required. On the other hand, one could argue (and this is reflected in the language used by scientists) that the relevant instrument in this case includes all the individual telescopes as well as the imaging algorithms. The relevant instrument is the telescope the size of the Earth. On the former reading, Elder suggests the EHT images would count as indirect; on the latter as direct.

The case is further complicated by the fact that we need to be more precise about *what* exactly the target phenomenon is: the black hole interior, exterior,

---

[29] See Galison et al. (2023) for a review of the various historical, philosophical and sociological concepts that the EHT collaboration raises.

or the event horizon (Doboszewski & Lehmkuhl, 2023, 13)? There are reasons why the interior of a black hole is in principle unobservable for an external observer: it is surrounded by an event horizon. If the EHT claims to have made a direct observation, it can surely only be of the exterior of the black hole, and specifically its effects on the surrounding materials in the form of accretion disks and jets. Of course, this suggest that it's plausible that *no* observation of a black hole will ever be direct. So be it. As Elder stresses, there is no reason why this should prevent us from learning a great deal about black holes from indirect observations anyway.

To conclude this discussion of direct detections of gravitational waves or black holes, I want to reiterate that none of the so-called direct observations are even remotely similar to observation with the naked eye. All of them heavily rely on instrumentation and various kinds of simulations. Doboszewski and Elder (2025) have recently analyzed the role of simulations in the LIGO/Virgo-results and in the EHT observations, and in what context these simulations lead to circular reasoning in the inferences drawn. I will return to the topic of computer simulations in Section 6.3.

5.3 'Indirect' Detection: Hawking Radiation and Analogue Experiments

It should be clear by now that black holes are notoriously hard to get empirical access to. The previous section described some features of black holes that can be detected through their effects on their environment, but there are other predicted features that are not detectable. One such a feature is Hawking radiation, a predicted black-body radiation emitted by black holes. This phenomenon is one of the most crucial predictions from black hole thermodynamics.[30] It is also much fainter than the CMB. This makes it unlikely that any human technology will ever be able to detect Hawking radiation. Evans and Thébault (2020) classify Hawking radiation therefore as 'unmanipulable and inaccessible (in practice)'.

Given that Hawking radiation is a cornerstone of black hole thermodynamics, physicists have tried to find ways around its inaccessibility: so-called analogue gravity experiments. Following an initial suggestion from Unruh (1981), these experiments aim to create 'dumb holes', manipulable systems that are similar to black holes such that one would expect an analogous effect to Hawking radiation to be observable in the manipulable system.[31] Since the

---

[30] The original derivation comes from Hawking (1975); for a recent philosophical summary of black hole thermodynamics, see Wallace (2018, 2019).
[31] See Thébault (2019) for a review of the various derivations.

first proposal, the field has grown significantly (Field, 2021a). But the hope still remains that one can learn about black holes from fairly straightforward laboratory experiments. This raises the question whether this hope is warranted, that is, whether analogue experiments can offer genuine confirmation for hypotheses about black holes or not.

Before looking at the question of confirmation, some more detail on what sets analogue experiments apart from regular experiments is needed. In what follows, the 'source system' refers to the experimental system that can be actively intervened on in the lab, and the 'target system' is the system one wants to draw conclusions about based on what is learned from the source system. According to Crowther, Linnemann, and Wüthrich (2021), what sets apart analogue experiments from more conventional experiments is that in conventional experiments, the source and target system are "supposed to be [...] the same kind of system for the purpose of interest" (S3709). In analogue experiments, the source and target system are similarly "supposed to be [...] the same kind of system, [...] [but the target system] is inaccessible under the relevant conditions for confirming that it is actually the same kind of system as [the source system] for the purpose of interest" (S3709-S3710). Thus, the main difference between conventional and analogue experiments is whether we have access to the target to ensure that it is of the same type as the source system.

Evans and Thébault (2020) push back against this definition by showing that the inaccessibility of a target does not automatically imply that it is impossible to draw any kind of inferences about that target. For instance, stellar interiors were confirmed to be of the same type as conventional laboratory systems in nuclear physics, despite stellar interiors being inaccessible. Instead, Evans and Thébault focus on the nature of the inference between source and target. While in conventional experiments source and target are assumed to be of the same type, this is not the case for analogue experiments. In analogue experiments, the source and target systems are of different-but-analogous types. More precisely, following Field (2021b): in analogue experiments, the source and target are of a different type at the micro-level, meaning that the modeling frameworks to describe their micro-level behaviors are distinct (e.g., gravity and fluid dynamics), but they nonetheless display similar macro-level behavior. It is because the source and target systems are of different micro-level types that the reliability of source to target requires a new kind of justification compared to regular experiments.

Field's classification clarifies why the question of confirmation is contentious for analogue experiments. The relation between source and target is one of analogy, and, as all authors in the literature agree, analogies are *not* confirmatory (Crowther et al., 2021; Dardashti, Thébault, and Winsberg, 2017; Field, 2021b).

Despite this difficulty, Dardashti et al. (2017) argue that analogue experiments can provide confirmation if the following conditions are met: the modeling frameworks for source and target systems are adequate within their respective domains, and the two frameworks are sufficiently similar such that there is an isomorphism between them within the relevant domains of applicability. In the case of analogue gravity experiments, they are confident that the isomorphism and the adequacy of the model of the source system are sufficiently established in the relevant domains of applicability. The difficulty lies in demonstrating the adequacy of the modeling framework for the black hole: how can this be established, given that scientists had to resort to analogue experiments due to the inaccessibility of black holes in the first place? Dardashti et al. argue that universality arguments can give reason to believe in the adequacy of the black hole modeling framework.

Crowther et al. (2021) take issue with this last step. They point out that these universality arguments assume that black holes can be modeled, as Hawking originally did, within semi-classical gravity. There are, however, well-known issues with this approach – not in the least the trans-Planckian problem (addressed by Crowther et al. 2021; Thébault 2019). Thus, Crowther et al. are concerned that the universality argument that is required for analogue experiments to be confirmatory assumes the adequacy of the modeling framework it is supposed to establish.

Building on a Bayesian analysis of analogue experiments from Dardashti et al. (2019), Field (2021b, Sec. 2.2.1) gives a more precise analysis of the circumstances under which analogue experiments can be genuinely confirmatory. Field shows that the conditions for genuine confirmation are very weak: it only requires that there is a universality argument with undetermined validity, and that there must be a chance that this universality argument is positively relevant to both the target and source system. Field thus agrees with Evans and Thébault (2020, Sec. 4.1.1) that denying the confirmatory power of analogue experiments collapses into inductive skepticism.

However, Field further shows that this does not imply that the confirmatory power of analogue experiments is significant. This because significance requires the universality argument to be *actually* positively relevant to both the target and the source system. And the problem in the case of analogue gravity experiments is that, as argued by Crowther et al. (2021), there is currently no such universality argument.

Field identifies two ways in which relevance of universality arguments can be established: either knowledge of the micro-structures of the target and source system reveal that they belong to the same universality class, or empirical tests of the macroscopic behavior of target and source reveal that they belong to the same universality class. It goes without saying that, as of right now, neither are available for black holes due to their current inaccessibility. Nonetheless, Field is hopeful that progress can be made – for example through the observations discussed in the previous sections, such that there is a future for analogue gravity experiments.

Two final notes are in order. First, Mathie (2023) gives a further argument in favor of the confirmatory power of analogue experiments. Mathie shows that the analogical inference between black holes and dumb holes that underpins analogue gravity experiments and the analogical inference underpinning black hole thermodynamics are crucially linked. This link suggests that there might be a tension between holding on to black hole thermodynamics and Hawking radiation on the one hand, and dismissing analogue gravity experiments on the other. Second, Field (2021a) argues that today, confirmation of hypotheses about inaccessible targets (black holes, but also the early universe) is no longer the sole focus of analogue experiments. Field identifies two new roles: exploring the behavior of analogue systems in themselves, as well as investigating whether certain phenomena, like Hawking radiation, generalize. Thus, while we should remain modest for now about the potential for analogue gravity experiments to affect our understanding of black holes, these new roles do suggest that laboratory experiments could play an interesting role more broadly in context of cosmology and astrophysics.

6 Empiricism, Epistemology, and Ethics

The previous four sections have introduced focal points for novel physics that emerge out of contemporary cosmology and astrophysics, and some aspects that warrant philosophical scrutiny. Next, I want to take a step back and examine the methodology of cosmology and astrophysics more generally. I highlighted in the introduction that cosmology and astrophysics push the boundaries of empirical science. We can now get precise about what features of the research process pose genuine epistemic challenges and what features are merely peculiarities without clear epistemic implications. What warrants the confidence in cosmology and astrophysics, and what limits to empiricist epistemology do these fields face?

I begin by rebutting a misconception that has been most famously argued by Hacking: that the lack of manipulation and 'active' experimentation makes astrophysics and, by extension, cosmology not a real science (Section 6.1). This rebuttal does not imply that cosmology and astrophysics do not face serious difficulties. First, there are certain limitations on their empirical basis – not due to the lack of experiment per se, but due to us only having empirical access to one universe, our particular vantage point within that universe, and the peculiarities of our home galaxy (Section 6.2). Second, cosmology and astrophysics require multiscale modeling at an unparalleled level. Connecting these different scales, both in terms of observations and simulations, brings a separate host of epistemic challenges (Section 6.3). Finally, cosmology, astrophysics, and astronomy all rely on telescope observations. Terrestrial observatories are situated in a broader sociological and environmental context. The ethical implications surrounding both the history of these disciplines as well as setting up new observatories are discussed in Section 6.4.

6.1 Refuting the Lack-of-Experiment Objection

One cannot put the universe, a galaxy, or a star in a lab. This obvious fact was taken to be a huge challenge for astronomy and astrophysics by Hacking (1989). Examining the case of gravitational lensing, Hacking argued that astrophysicists merely construct various "models upon models upon models" (576). This abundance of models was, according to Hacking, symptomatic of a broader issue: these models allow astrophysicists to "save the phenomena" (577). By contrast, the aim of natural science is "manipulating and interfering with the world in order to understand it" (577). Indeed, Hacking argued that natural sciences "came into being" when they adopted the experimental method. Since astronomy's methods haven't changed since ancient times, astronomy is therefore "not a natural science at all" (577).[32] While Hacking's phrasing might be polemic, it is plausible that the objection can have some intuitive appeal. Surely, the lack of experiment poses a serious challenge?

All aspects of Hacking's argument have garnered significant push-back. Shapere (1993) rebuts Hacking's review of gravitational lensing, both in terms of scientific content and in terms of it being a very young research area when Hacking first described it. Anderl (2016) points out that the use of models is ubiquitous in all of science. But most focus has gone to Hacking's dismissal of astrophysics as a science due to the lack of intervention, which Anderl (2016, 657) helpfully frames as a concern about underdetermination: is it the case that a lack of intervention means that astrophysics is more susceptible to

---

[32] Although this phrase will strike most readers as dismissive and negative, it's not entirely clear that Hacking himself thought of it as such. In a review paper of philosophy of experiment from one year earlier, Hacking denounces the Baconian philosophy of experiment that focuses on mastering nature (Hacking, 1988). Instead, Hacking expresses the hope that "the image of the future [of philosophizing about experiment] will be one of the experimenter collaborating with nature rather than mastering it" (154). This is reflected in astrophysics, which Hacking still calls "scarcely a laboratory science at all" (154).

concerns about underdetermination and hence can only ever hope to save the phenomena?

At least three strategies have been used to respond to the underdetermination concern: (i) argue that astrophysics does make use of experiments along Hacking's own criteria (Boyd, 2023; Sandell, 2010) – sometimes combined with pointing out that 'use' of entities in research and 'intervention' on said entities are not obviously co-extensive (Doboszewski & Lehmkuhl, 2023; Shapere, 1993); (ii) accept, sometimes implicitly, the observation/experiment distinction as epistemically significant but argue that the lack of experiment can be overcome without implying a loss in scientific status – this response is either explicitly linked to or mirrors discussions about the epistemology of historical sciences more generally (Anderl, 2016; Elder, 2023b, 2024); and (iii) argue that the distinction between experiment-qua-physical-intervention on the one hand, and observation on the other cannot serve as a guide for epistemic judgments (Boyd & Matthiessen, 2024).

As an example of the first strategy, Boyd (2023) discusses cases from the field of 'laboratory astrophysics'. Examples include dark matter production experiments and analogue black hole experiments, but also spectroscopy, accelerator-based nuclear astrophysics, and laboratory supernova research, Boyd's main case study. Laboratory astrophysics should, according to Hacking's classification, be a contradiction-in-terms. Boyd counters that:

> What makes astrophysics *astrophysics* is that it investigates the nature of celestial objects and processes using a suite of resources from physics. And what makes laboratory astrophysics *laboratory* astrophysics, is that it carries out such investigations using terrestrial experiments. (Boyd, 2023, 17)

Boyd argues that the inference from the terrestrial experiment to the target system out in space happens through the usual argument for the external validity of an experiment, that is, by arguing that the states probed in the lab and those instantiated by the astrophysical systems are tokens of the same type (23-25). If successful, it seems that there is no reason to be more concerned about underdetermination in laboratory astrophysics than in other experimental sciences, thus undermining Hacking's argument.

Interestingly enough, Boyd argues that in the case under discussion, the external validity arguments actually fail. However, Boyd stresses that this would not have become clear if one stayed focused on framing the experiment as 'experimental' and therefore 'epistemically better'. Indeed, a corollary of this first strategy is that, sometimes, observations are better suited for a particular research question. For instance, Elder (2023a) points out that LIGO/Virgo is able to probe novel regimes of general relativity, even though there is a clear lack of manipulation (see also Elder 2025). A nice example of how observations have informed realistic models of the interior of stars is discussed by Suárez (2023). In modern particle physics, the first empirical evidence for the existence of neutrinos came from observations of the Sun. And the universe is thanks to Zel'dovich more generally known as the 'poor man's accelerator', because the early universe and stellar interiors can reach energy scales that can never be recreated in terrestrial experiments.

What about the second strategy? Anderl (2016) connects the concerns about underdetermination to a debate about historical sciences. Historical sciences aim to reconstruct causal chains that led to current observations without any intervening on that hypothesized causal chain. Anderl's response to the underdetermination concern is twofold. First, Anderl follows Cleland's (2002) argument that stereotypical historical science uses the so-called Sherlock-Holmes strategy: find a causal explanation that can unify all observed traces, and discriminate between competing explanations using 'smoking gun' evidence. The lack of experiment is no reason to be concerned about underdetermination, because of the time-asymmetry of causation, Cleland continues: one cause can generate a range of traces, of which only a subset can be sufficient to identify the original cause. Anderl agrees with Cleland's conclusion that it's not obvious that underdetermination due to unidentified auxiliaries in experimental settings is in any way less strong than underdetermination due to multiple explanations for traces in observational settings. Thus, while it is the case that astrophysicists cannot actively recreate causal chains in the lab, it is not obvious that that creates a significant epistemic hurdle compared to experimental sciences.

Second, Anderl points out that not all types of astrophysical research are stereotypically historical science. While some research questions are about reconstructing the causal history of singular events, a lot of astrophysics aims to make general statements about types of objects, from main-sequence stars to Type II supernovae or elliptical galaxies.[33] The universe contains a lot of instances of each of these classes: it constitutes a "cosmic laboratory" (Anderl, 2016, Section 3.2). Because astrophysicists can observe so many instances of the same type, they can at the very least run 'quasi-experiments'. Quasi-experiments compare a control and test group which are not randomly assigned. They therefore require the use of statistical tools and simulations to draw any conclusions. Similar to the first part of Anderl's argument, I believe it's safe

---

[33] This part of Anderl's argument does not obviously extend to cosmology, where the general focus is reconstructing the causal history of our singular universe.

both introduced to account for observations in regimes far beyond where the background theories like general relativity have been tested. Smeenk and Ellis (2017) argue that this introduces a new type of underdetermination: how do we know whether the proposed alterations are not masking that the background theory needs to be modified? This assessment has to happen on a case-by-case basis.

6.2.2 Cosmic Variance

Cosmology, unlike astrophysics, deals with a unique target: there is only one universe that we have empirical access to. However, many predictions that are derived from ΛCDM are statistical in nature – most famously the CMB. That means that when the observed universe shows features that deviate from those statistical predictions, there is an open question whether these features are merely a statistical fluke, or whether they are genuine anomalies that warrant modifying ΛCDM (Smeenk & Ellis, 2017). Examples include the cold spot in the CMB and the fine-tuning problems solved by inflation (Section 2.1). Note that this challenge does not arise as commonly in astrophysics because the universe often produces several instances of the same type of object (Anderl, 2016).

6.2.3 The Cosmological Principle

ΛCDM represents the evolution of the universe at the largest scale by employing (perturbed) FLRW-models. As explained in Section 1.2, these models are solutions to the Einstein Field Equations if one assumes the so-called Cosmological Principle, that is, that the universe is homogeneous and isotropic at the largest scales. But how is this cosmological principle justified as applicable to our actual universe?[34]

Smeenk (2020) argues that the best justification is through the assumption of the so-called Copernican principle as constitutive to the pursuit of physical cosmology. The Copernican principle, in Smeenk's preferred formulation, is a claim about evidence: "we can plausibly take some types of observations as a representative sample from an ensemble of possible observations" (Smeenk, 2020, 224). In other words, the Copernican principle posits that cosmological observations are not biased by our specific presence in a particular place in the universe as observers (the exception here are observations affected by cosmic

---

[34] The Cosmological Principle has itself been a topic of heated philosophical debate, and its formulation is tricky. I won't be able to discuss this debate in much detail here. I See Earman (1995) on the huge inductive generalization it requires and Manchak (2011) and references therein on the impossibility to establish global isotropy.

variance). If we accept the Copernican principle, Smeenk argues, there are certain theoretical results that imply the homogeneity of the universe based on the observed isotropy of the CMB. And we should accept the antecedent here because the Copernican principle is "a constitutive principle for the pursuit of physical cosmology" (225). In other words, if we do not accept the Copernican principle, there is no point to physical cosmology, that is, cosmology as an empirical science, at all: all of our evidence would *only* be representative of our local environment, providing no inductive basis for global inferences whatsoever.

6.2.4 The Typicality of the Milky Way

As mentioned before, the challenge of a unique vantage point on a unique object is less pressing for astrophysics than for cosmology. However, there is still an analogous problem to cosmic variance. Namely, most detailed observations of the interior structure of a galaxy or a galactic halo are based on observations of the Milky Way (sometimes supplemented with observations of Andromeda, our closest neighboring galaxy in the Local Group). But how do we know whether the Milky Way is a representative instance of the disk-galaxy population? This question becomes even more pressing in light of the small-scale challenges to ΛCDM, discrepancies between predictions and observations on (sub-)galactic scales (see Section 3.3). However, it is impossible to determine whether these inconsistencies are genuine anomalies if we don't know whether the Milky Way observations generalize. Doing so unwarrantedly, risks introducing a "Copernican bias" (Aragon-Calvo, Silk, and Neyrinck, 2022).

For example, Licquia, Newman, and Bershady (2016) investigate whether the Milky Way obeys typical galactic scaling relations like the Tully-Fisher relation, which links a galaxy's mass to its luminosity. With regard to the Tully-Fisher relation, they find the Milky Way to by typical and therefore suggest that "it is a suitable laboratory for studying the driving mechanism of the relation" (13). But success in one area does not imply success everywhere. The same study further concludes that the Milky Way is unusually compact for a spiral galaxy based on the scaling relation between luminosity, rotational velocity, and galaxy size. They suggest that this might be due to the Milky Way having an unusual history, which may also have affected the population of satellite galaxies around the Milky Way (11).

Efforts are underway to determine the typicality of the Milky Way. One recent strategy is the study of so-called 'Milky Way Analogues' (MWAs), galaxies outside of the Local Group that are in some respect or other similar to the Milky Way (although note that there are multiple ways of defining MWAs, see Boardman et al. 2020). For example, the SAGA survey (Geha et al., 2017;

Mao et al., 2021) studies the satellite galaxy populations around MWAs to determine how representative the satellite populations in the Local Group – including the Milky Way – are of galaxy evolution more generally. But, as the example shows, so far there don't seem to be principled grounds to determine which features of the Milky Way generalize and which ones don't.

6.3 Multi-Scale Modeling

The previous section discussed challenges that arise due to our limited vantage point on a single universe. There is a separate set of challenges that relates to multi-scale modeling. Cosmology and astrophysics aim to model systems across large ranges of length- and timescales. While the relevant physics is largely deterministic, unlike, for example, in climate science where human decision-making is relevant, the range of scales raises significant hurdles.

6.3.1 Combining Observations at Different Scales

A first challenge emerges in combining parameter estimates from measurements at different scales. ΛCDM has at least six free parameters that need to be determined through observations, from the baryon density parameter to the spectral index of the of the CMB power spectrum. There are usually multiple ways of setting these (and other, derived) parameter values, which are commonly classified as 'local' (for smaller scales) or 'global' (for the largest scales, like the CMB). As Smeenk (2020, 223) points out, "[a]ccepting the ΛCDM model brings with it a commitment to account for how the parameters determined via "global" measurements of the [CMB] relate to the "local" measurements of these same parameters". This is a nontrivial commitment, it turns out.

One of the key parameters in cosmology is the Hubble parameter H_0, which measures the current expansion rate of the universe. In 2001, the Hubble Space Telescope Key Project resolved a decades-long debate by setting its value to $H_0 = 72 \pm 8 \text{ km s}^{-1} \text{ Mpc}^{-1}$ (Freedman et al., 2001). This value was based on local measurements, for instance observations of supernova redshifts, but it was also consistent with global determinations of H_0 at the time. However, since this milestone result, a new tension has begun to arise between the local and global determinations, with the difference between the two reaching significant levels. Gueguen (2023) analyzes the case in detail and shows that there are currently insufficient reasons to believe that the Hubble tension is, indeed, a crisis. Gueguen ties this into discussions about robustness and replication (see also Matarese & McCoy 2024), and argues that the key to resolving the crisis one way or another lies in tracking the unknown systematic errors. Note, however, that if this tension does persist, it would undermine one of the key assumptions of ΛCDM about how measurements at different scales are related.

Another challenge for multiscale modeling efforts comes in the form of the 'snapshot problem' (Jacquart 2020, see also Anderl 2016, 623, Smeenk & Gallagher 2020, 1223-1224): most astrophysical objects tend to evolve on much longer timescales than humans have been observing them. This means that when astrophysicists model the evolution of, say, a main-sequence star, they cannot test their model by observing one single star's evolution. Instead, they observe many different stars that are assumed to be in different stages of that evolution and that therefore give 'snapshot' images of that evolution. Or, similarly, they observe stars at higher redshifts, which are in an earlier stage of their evolution, and stars at lower redshifts, which are in a later stage. Connecting these snapshots into a single evolutionary story requires complex modeling and computer simulations.

6.3.2 The Epistemology of Computer Simulations

Simulations fulfill several crucial roles in cosmology and astrophysics (Anderl, 2016; De Baerdemaeker & Boyd, 2020; Jacquart, 2020; Massimi, 2018; Smeenk & Gallagher, 2020). They connect snapshots into a full causal history, but they also enable deriving predictions from ΛCDM for multiple scales.

Usually, cosmological computer simulations model the structure formation of the universe as described by ΛCDM at the largest scales. While early simulations tended to solely model the gravitational interaction of dark matter (dominant at the largest scales), more recent simulations also include so-called hydrodynamic processes like stellar winds and supernova feedback. These processes may take place at a smaller scale, sometimes even below the simulation resolution, but they are nonetheless expected to have an effect on structure formation at larger scales. Because of the inclusion of such nonlinear physics, simulations require the inclusion of numerical methods to solve the model equations. Given their central role in scientific practice, the question arises how the reliability of these simulations can be established (a challenge that is not unique to cosmology and astrophysics). After all, if the only way scientists can create a story out of singular snapshots or derive predictions from ΛCDM is through simulations, it is crucial to determine that that story is accurate.

What makes it hard to establish the reliability of simulations is the fact that they are epistemically opaque. Smeenk and Gallagher (2020) identify three different types of opacity: (i) opacity due to the intractability of the full range of calculations involved in the simulation; (ii) opacity due to the inability to assign blame to a particular module of the simulation when something goes wrong. In particular, while different simulation modules may be responsible for modeling specific physical processes, stitching them together often requires ad hoc fixes to ensure the simulation behaves smoothly; and (iii) opacity due to the ability to tune the free parameters of a simulation to generate the desired output without having a handle on what these parameters represent. Given these different sources of opacity, what techniques can be employed to ensure the reliability of the simulations?

A first option is the so-called 'validation and verification'-ideal. According to this ideal, the reliability of a simulation could only be established by strictly separating whether the simulation accurately solves the model equations through its numerical methods (verification) and whether the simulation outputs are an accurate representation of the target phenomenon (validation) (Kadowaki, 2023). Verification has to be complete before any validation can be achieved. However, Kadowaki (2023) argues based on a survey of tests of astrophysical magneto-hydrodynamical simulations that this ideal is not satisfied in practice, and indeed, that it doesn't *need* to be satisfied.

Another strategy would be to benchmark simulation outputs to another reliable source (Smeenk & Gallagher, 2020). Gueguen (n.d., 3) lists three kinds of benchmarks as the main strategies for assessing the reliability of astrophysical and computer simulations: comparing the outputs to (semi-)analytic solutions, comparing the outputs to observations, and comparing the outputs to other numerical results (either through convergence studies or code comparisons).

The first two types of benchmarks, analytic solutions to the fundamental equations of the simulated model and empirical data that was not used in constructing the simulation (i.e., data that the simulation was not tuned to match), would be ideal. The problem is that these strategies are "frustratingly rare" (Smeenk & Gallagher, 2020, 1228). Indeed, the reason why simulations are used is usually that the required calculations are intractable, and because the required data are rare – recall the snapshot problem.

But perhaps one could use other simulation outputs as a benchmark. One version of this comes in the form of "convergence studies". As Gueguen (2020) explains, the basic idea is the following. Simulations contain a lot of numerical parameters that are completely unconstrained. To determine whether the value of these parameters have an effect on the simulation output, their values are systematically varied in a series of simulation runs. This then gives information about the range of parameter values for which the simulation output is unaffected by the parameter. These ranges form so-called 'convergence criteria' under which the simulation outputs are robust.

Gueguen (2020) shows that there are reasons to be skeptical about convergence being an indicator of the reliability of simulation outputs. First, convergence is not sufficient for establishing reliability, because it can sometimes be the case that there is convergence on two independent regions of parameter space without any reason to believe one region is the 'real' output. Second, convergence can sometimes be the result of numerical artefacts. Thus, robustness in the form of convergence studies does not suffice to establish the reliability of numerical simulation outputs.

Another way of using simulations as benchmarks is through so-called code comparisons. In code comparisons, different simulations are compared with one another to find invariant features across simulations. At face value, this allows for a much stronger form of robustness because the robustness is now across different simulations, with different assumptions and artefacts (Gueguen, n.d.). Are code comparisons indeed a more promising strategy for assessing the reliability of computer simulations?

Gueguen (n.d.) argues that there are still concerns to be had about code comparisons. First, Gueguen identifies a practical issue that in order for code comparisons to allow for a strong robustness argument, the ensemble of codes used should span the range of possibilities as much as possible. In practice, such an ideal ensemble is almost never achieved. Sometimes not all coding teams are willing to participate. Even if all teams would participate, the available codes often don't constitute an 'ideal ensemble'. That is, the available simulations span only a small range of the possible ways to simulate a target because of practical limitations. Codes often build on one another or use the same simplifying assumptions to improve computability. Because these assumptions are shared across codes, they are never put to the test themselves (Gallagher & Smeenk, 2023; Smeenk & Gallagher, 2020).

Second, Gueguen (n.d.) shows that there is an in principle tension blocking the formulation of strong robustness arguments based on code comparisons. Gueguen identifies two requirements for a successful code comparison project: comparability and minimal diversity. Comparability requires that the simulations aim to model similar targets using the same physics. The motivation for this requirement is fairly obvious: it is necessary to even permit comparisons between codes in the first place. Diversity requires that "the common assumptions used in the ensemble must not be possible generators of artifacts" (19). The idea is that if there is agreement between the codes, it must be ensured that the agreement is not due to artifacts but that it tracks a real physical effect predicted by the underlying physical model(s).

Reviewing two recent code comparison projects, AGORA and AQUILA, Gueguen (n.d.) shows that the two aforementioned requirements are in tension with one another. Namely, in order to make different codes – codes which implement different types of sub-grid physics with different modeling assumptions and numerical parameters – comparable to one another, minimal diversity is so significantly violated that no robustness argument can be warranted anymore. Thus, Gueguen concludes, while code comparisons can be useful in various ways, these projects currently do not warrant any conclusions about the reliability of the simulation outputs that the codes generated.

While my discussion of computer simulations may suggest pessimism about assessing the reliability of simulations, I think this would be the wrong lesson to draw. Rather, the philosophical work discussed here shows that there is an important role for philosophers of science to play when it comes to state-of-the-art scientific practice. By analyzing the epistemology of the various strategies discussed, philosophers can, on the one hand, improve their own epistemology of computer simulations and on the other, help improve scientific methodology. As an instance of the latter, Meskhidze (2023) chronicles a code comparison project where philosophers were actively involved in the project. Aware of Gueguen's criticism, the group adjusted the aims and methodology of the code comparison project. For one, the scope of their project was *not* to establish the reliability of their simulation outputs in general. Instead, their goal was to investigate whether differences in implementation of self-interacting dark matter would affect their simulation output. This question could be answered with quite high certainty, revealing more details about the functioning of the specific simulations along the way. I take Meskhidze's case study exemplary of how philosophers can contribute fruitfully to scientific research (see also Godard Palluet & Gueguen 2024).

6.4 The Ethics of Cosmology and Astrophysics

Philosophers should not just contribute to epistemological debates in cosmology and astrophysics. Another equally, if not more, important task is to participate in ethical debates about these disciplines. A naive view may suggest that cosmology and astrophysics would be morally good or at the very least neutral (who could be harmed by observations of stars?). This is far from the truth. Cosmology and astrophysics do not operate in a vacuum. They are human endeavors practiced in a particular sociopolitical, historical, and environmental context (de Swart, Thresher, and Argüelles, 2024). For instance, the fact that these disciplines are becoming more and more computationally expensive raises questions about their climate impact and how to mitigate it. Cosmology and astrophysics (and astronomy) also have a long history of entanglement with colonialism and oppression (Prescod-Weinstein, 2021).

The 1919 eclipse expedition that provided key evidence for general relativity was enabled by the combined colonial powers of Britain and Portugal (Simões & Sousa, 2019). And even the newly accepted model of the expanding universe was appropriated by some to defend white settler colonialism in the 1930s (Schneider & De Baerdemaeker, 2023).

Arguably one of the most complex issues is the siting of new earth-based telescopes. In a recent podcast episode, Thresher summarizes various challenges associated with telescope siting (Enander & Thresher, 2024). The following discussion is largely drawn from that episode.[35] Optimal observing conditions for telescopes require remote locations at high elevation. That usually implies culturally significant mountain tops with delicate ecosystems in countries with a history of colonization. Building new telescopes thus comes with environmental, cultural, political, and socioeconomic impact.

With regard to environmental impact, Thresher highlights that telescope construction commonly implies disturbing unique ecosystems. For example, Mount Graham in Arizona, home to three telescopes, is also home to the endangered Mt. Graham red squirrel (Swanner, 2013).[36] Moreover, the construction of ultra-clean detectors and mirrors often generates large amounts of waste. Decommissioning is an even more delicate exercise (the environmental impact study for decommissioning the Arecibo telescope in Puerto Rico (NSF, 2017) gives a good sense). In the past, there often were no clear plans for decommissioning telescopes that had reached the end of their lifetime, thus leaving enormous structures to slowly decay and further destroy the environment. Responsibly decommissioning telescopes comes with a hefty price tag. 'Dealing with the issue once it arises' is clearly not an option when the cost is that high.

Culturally, Thresher points out that telescopes are often constructed on mountains that are culturally significant for local and indigenous communities. These communities have historically not been heard in the construction of previous telescopes, which tends to create a deep sense of mistrust towards new telescope projects. This is closely tied to the political impact of telescope construction. Many telescope sites are in regions with a history of colonization or oppression. Consider, for instance, the case of Chile, one of the prime locations for Earth-based telescopes. The European Space Organization (ESO) runs various telescopes in the Atacama Desert, including the Very Large Telescope,

---

[35] I'm also grateful to the Responsible Siting Reading Group, organized by Helen Meskhidze, for valuable discussions on these topics.

[36] See Swanner (2013, Ch. 5) for a detailed reconstruction of the competing narratives that emerged between astronomy, ecology, and Apache culture in the controversy about telescope building on Mt. Graham.

and the future (not very creatively named) Extremely Large Telescope. In the 1990s, the construction of the Very Large Telescope became imperiled due to legal disputes: the land on which it was to be constructed was claimed to be private land which had unjustly been donated in the 1970s to ESO by Pinochet, Chile's former dictator, whose regime was notorious for its human rights violations (Long, 1994).

Finally, Thresher describes the socioeconomic impact of telescopes. Modern telescopes represent the cutting edge of human technology, but they are rarely accessible to people living nearby. Instead, the use of telescopes is a privilege for international scientists, who can fly in for a short observing run or even run their observations remotely. Local communities are historically only offered less-prestigious technical or janitorial job opportunities. Meanwhile, credit for new discoveries tends to go to research scientists, much less to the technical staff.

The case of the Thirty Meter Telescope (TMT) at the Maunakea[37] peak in Hawai'i provides an example of how all of these factors can come to a head. Maunakea is one of the best locations for Earth-based astronomy in the Northern hemisphere, due to its remote location and stable atmosphere. It has been developed for astronomy since the second half of the twentieth century, but the mountain is sacred for native Hawaiians.[38] The construction of the TMT, which would be larger than any existing telescope on the peak, has been continuously opposed, protested, and blocked by native Hawaiians. While the conflict has often been unhelpfully framed as one of 'science vs. religion', the truth is much more nuanced: it is about a history of colonization, environmental impact, a lack of respect for indigenous rights, questions about informed consent, and the assumption that scientific progress can come at all costs. Maunakea is a prime example of how intricately tied telescopes are to the context in which they are constructed, and how ignoring that context can significantly harm both people and science. Thresher implores that reckoning with that context and making morally informed choices is crucial for the future of cosmology and astrophysics and for a just science.

---

[37] The one-word spelling "Maunakea" is recommended by The University of Hawai'i at Hilo College of Hawaiian Language, Ka Haka 'Ula o Ke'elikōlani. See https://hilo.hawaii.edu/maunakea/culture/meaning.

[38] The history of astronomy on the Maunakea and the TMT dispute is far too complex for me to review it here. Swanner (2013, 2017) gives a historical introduction to the debate. Kahanamoku et al. (2020); Prescod-Weinstein et al. (2020) give concrete recommendations for how to move forward. The second season of the *Offshore* podcast covers the Maunakea controversy; see https://www.offshorepodcast.org/episodes/mauna-kea/.

Recent efforts have shown that things can get better. The next generation Event Horizon Telescope (ngEHT) collaboration includes a responsible siting working group. This working group is tasked with developing guidelines for how to site a new telescope without causing harms in any of the aforementioned ways. One of the central questions is to understand what 'informed consent' can look like when it comes to siting a new telescope, if it is at all possible in a given historical context. The group consists of philosophers of science, ethicists, sociologists, anthropologists, astronomers, and more. By recognizing that responsible siting is key to the future of cosmology and astrophysics, and by actively calling on the expertise of humanities scholars and social scientists, the ngEHT hopes the avoid the harms that have often been done in the name of science.

7 Conclusion

The progress cosmology, astrophysics, and astronomy have made over the last century has been remarkable. Until the mid-1920s, it was still up for debate as to whether the universe extended beyond the Milky Way, and the idea of an expanding universe still seemed a mathematical folly to many. The current concordance model seems light-years ahead – especially given the fact that it includes entities like dark matter and dark energy, and the possibility of a phase of cosmic inflation. Yet, those examples of novel physics also pose a challenge. Given that our main point of access to cosmic inflation or dark energy is the universe at the largest scales, how much empirical progress can we expect to make on them? How can scientists gather more empirical data about black holes or dark matter, entities that are inhospitable to empirical observation through the electromagnetic spectrum – still our prime window on the universe?

Despite these challenges, I do not believe the main lesson of this Element is skepticism about research in cosmology, astrophysics, and astronomy. Rather, as the different sections have shown, the nature of scientific research has successfully adapted to the circumstances, despite the many roadblocks along the way. New empirical and theoretical probes, from analogue experiments to computer simulations, are continuously being developed. This also means that there are unique opportunities for philosophers of science.

Philosophy of science stands to learn a lot about the epistemology and metaphysics of science from these fields. The inflationary multiverse and dark matter provide interesting test cases for different versions of scientific realism. The distinction between experiments and observations, and between direct and indirect observations, can be better scrutinized (and perhaps rejected). Various limitations on the role of robustness reasoning have emerged. And the epistemology of historical sciences may need to be reassessed to account for astrophysical and cosmological practice.

More generally, the survey I have provided shows that the philosophical literature on astrophysics (and to a lesser extent cosmology) has skewed to focusing on cases of 'exotic' physics, like black holes or dark matter.[39] Much less attention has been paid to scientific research about 'regular' stars or galaxies. I can see two possible explanations for this bias. First, it might be that these exotic cases generate the most exciting philosophical puzzles, for example, related to 'unobservability' or 'underdetermination'. The bias in the literature is then a result of the fact that these areas of research are the most philosophically interesting, while comparatively little can be gleaned from more 'ordinary' astrophysics.

I doubt that this is actually the case, however. Instead, I think the following explanation is more plausible. Namely, in those more 'exotic' research contexts like dark energy research or black hole research, the challenges that cosmology and astrophysics more generally face (e.g., the lack of intervention, our unique vantage point) become glaring, often because they are compounded with additional challenges (e.g., the lack of electromagnetic signals). This makes the general challenges that cosmology and astrophysics face even more biting. But this also means that if a case can be made for scientific progress being possible even in the most difficult of circumstances – as I have tried to do in this Element, the epistemology of cosmology and astrophysics is more generally strengthened. Still, while this might be a good initial tendency, I also believe that the philosophical literature on cosmology and astrophysics is incomplete as long as this bias remains.

Finally, cosmologists, astrophysicists, and astronomers are often grappling with questions that philosophers can provide guidance on. One returning issue is the demarcation problem, and to what extent falsifiability can be a useful criterion for science. Whether or not underdetermination is pernicious or not, as well as the different kinds of underdetermination that occur, has been discussed extensively in the philosophical literature. And, finally, cosmology and astrophysics have only recently begun to recognize the ethical aspects of their research. Here, philosophical reflection can be paramount to improving scientific practice.

Thus, throughout this Element, I have identified areas for cross-pollination between scientific practice and philosophy. In some areas, this has already led to fruitful collaborations. More is sure to come.

---

[39] I am grateful to an anonymous reviewer for raising this point.

References

Abbott, B., Abbott, R., Abbott, T., et al., Observation of Gravitational Waves from a Binary Black Hole Merger. *Physical Review Letters*, *116*(6), 061102. https://doi.org/10.1103/PhysRevLett.116.061102.

Abelson, S. S. (2022a, February). The Fate of Tensor-Vector-Scalar Modified Gravity. *Foundations of Physics*, *52*(1), 31. https://doi.org/10.1007/s10701-022-00545-1.

Abelson, S. S. (2022b, August). Variety of Evidence in Multimessenger Astronomy. *Studies in History and Philosophy of Science*, *94*, 133–142. https://doi.org/10.1016/j.shpsa.2022.05.006.

Allzén, S. (2021, December). Scientific Realism and Empirical Confirmation: A Puzzle. *Studies in History and Philosophy of Science Part A*, *90*, 153–159. https://doi.org/10.1016/j.shpsa.2021.10.008.

Allzén, S. (2023). Extragalactic Reality Revisited: Astrophysics and Entity Realism. In N. Mills Boyd, S. De Baerdemaeker, K. Heng, & V. Matarese (Eds.), *Philosophy of Astrophysics* (Vol. 472, pp. 277–293). Cham: Springer International. (Series Title: Synthese Library) https://doi.org/10.1007/978-3-031-26618-8_15.

Anderl, S. (2016, April). Astronomy and Astrophysics. In P. Humphreys (Ed.), *The Oxford Handbook of Philosophy of Science* (Vol. 1, pp. 652-670). New York: Oxford University Press. https://doi.org/10.1093/oxfordhb/9780199368815.013.45.

Antoniou, A. (2023, July). Robustness and Dark-Matter Observation. *Philosophy of Science*, *90*(3), 629–647. https://doi.org/10.1017/psa.2023.50.

Aragon-Calvo, M. A., Silk, J., & Neyrinck, M. (2022, December). The Unusual Milky Way-Local Sheet System: Implications for Spin Strength and Alignment. *Monthly Notices of the Royal Astronomical Society: Letters*, *520*(1), L28–L32. https://doi.org/10.1093/mnrasl/slac161.

Avni, Y., & Bahcall, J. N. (1975, May). Ellipsoidal Light Variations and Masses of X-ray Binaries. *The Astrophysical Journal*, *197*, 675. https://doi.org/10.1086/153558.

Baade, W. (1956, February). The Period-Luminosity Relation of the Cepheids. *Publications of the Astronomical Society of the Pacific*, *68*, 5. (ADS Bibcode: 1956PASP...68....5B) https://doi.org/10.1086/126870.

Bekenstein, J., & Milgrom, M. (1984, November). Does the Missing Mass Problem Signal the Breakdown of Newtonian Gravity? *The Astrophysical Journal*, *286*, 7. https://doi.org/10.1086/162570.

Belot, G. (2023). *Accelerating Expansion: Philosophy and Physics with a Positive Cosmological Constant* (1st ed.). Oxford: Oxford University Press. https://doi.org/10.1093/oso/9780192866462.001.0001.

Benétreau-Dupin, Y. (2015, December). Blurring Out Cosmic Puzzles. *Philosophy of Science*, *82*(5), 879–891. https://doi.org/10.1086/683326.

Boardman, N., Zasowski, G., Newman, J. A., et al. (2020, September). Are the Milky Way and Andromeda Unusual? A Comparison with Milky Way and Andromeda Analogues. *Monthly Notices of the Royal Astronomical Society*, *498*(4), 4943–4954. https://doi.org/10.1093/mnras/staa2731.

Boyd, N. M. (2023). Laboratory Astrophysics: Lessons for Epistemology of Astrophysics. In N. Mills Boyd, S. De Baerdemaeker, K. Heng, & V. Matarese (Eds.), *Philosophy of Astrophysics* (Vol. 472, pp. 13–32). Cham: Springer International. (Series Title: Synthese Library) https://doi.org/10.1007/978-3-031-26618-8_2.

Boyd, N. M., De Baerdemaeker, S., Heng, K., & Matarese, V. (Eds.). (2023). *Philosophy of Astrophysics: Stars, Simulations, and the Struggle to Determine What is Out There* (Vol. 472). Cham: Springer International. https://doi.org/10.1007/978-3-031-26618-8.

Boyd, N. M., & Matthiessen, D. (2024, January). Observations, Experiments, and Arguments for Epistemic Superiority in Scientific Methodology. *Philosophy of Science*, *91*(1), 111–131. https://doi.org/10.1017/psa.2023.101.

Brandenberger, R. (2017, January). Initial Conditions for Inflation - A Short Review. *International Journal of Modern Physics D*, *26*(01), 1740002. (arXiv:1601.01918 [astro-ph, physics:gr-qc, physics:hep-ph, physics:hep-th]) https://doi.org/10.1142/S0218271817400028.

Brandenberger, R. (2019, May). Is the Spectrum of Gravitational Waves the "Holy Grail" of Inflation? *The European Physical Journal C*, *79*(5), 387. https://doi.org/10.1140/epjc/s10052-019-6883-4.

Bullock, J. S., & Boylan-Kolchin, M. (2017, August). Small-Scale Challenges to the ΛCDM Paradigm. *Annual Review of Astronomy and Astrophysics*, *55*(1), 343–387. (arXiv:1707.04256 [astro-ph, physics:hep-ph]) https://doi.org/10.1146/annurev-astro-091916-055313.

Chakravartty, A. (2017). "Scientific Realism". In Edward N. Zalta (ed.), The Stanford Encyclopedia of Philosophy. https://plato.stanford.edu/archives/sum2017/entries/scientific-realism/.

Ćirković, M. M., & Perović, S. (2018, May). Alternative Explanations of the Cosmic Microwave Background: A Historical and an Epistemological Perspective. *Studies in History and Philosophy of Science Part B: Studies in History and Philosophy of Modern Physics*, *62*, 1–18. https://doi.org/10.1016/j.shpsb.2017.04.005.

Cleland, C. E. (2002, September). Methodological and Epistemic Differences between Historical Science and Experimental Science. *Philosophy of Science*, *69*(3), 474–496. https://doi.org/10.1086/342455.

Clowe, D., Bradac, M., Gonzalez, A. H., et al. (2006, September). A Direct Empirical Proof of the Existence of Dark Matter. *The Astrophysical Journal*, *648*(2), L109–L113. (arXiv:astro-ph/0608407) https://doi.org/10.1086/508162.

Collins, H. M. (2017). *Gravity's Kiss: The Detection of Gravitational Waves*. Cambridge, MA: The MIT Press. (OCLC: 971118994).

Crowther, K., Linnemann, N. S., & Wüthrich, C. (2021, July). What We Cannot Learn from Analogue Experiments. *Synthese*, *198*(S16), 3701–3726. https://doi.org/10.1007/s11229-019-02190-0.

Curiel, E. (2019, January). The Many Definitions of a Black Hole. *Nature Astronomy*, *3*(1), 27–34. https://doi.org/10.1038/s41550-018-0602-1.

Currie, A. (2015, March). Marsupial Lions and Methodological Omnivory: Function, Success and Reconstruction in Paleobiology. *Biology & Philosophy*, *30*(2), 187–209. https://doi.org/10.1007/s10539-014-9470-y.

Currie, A. (2018). *Rock, Bone, and Ruin: An Optimist's Guide to the Historical Sciences*. Cambridge: The MIT Press. https://doi.org/10.7551/mitpress/11421.001.0001.

Dardashti, R., Hartmann, S., Thébault, K., & Winsberg, E. (2019, August). Hawking Radiation and Analogue Experiments: A Bayesian Analysis. *Studies in History and Philosophy of Science Part B: Studies in History and Philosophy of Modern Physics*, *67*, 1–11. https://doi.org/10.1016/j.shpsb.2019.04.004.

Dardashti, R., Thébault, K. P. Y., & Winsberg, E. (2017, March). Confirmation via Analogue Simulation: What Dumb Holes Could Tell Us about Gravity. *The British Journal for the Philosophy of Science*, *68*(1), 55–89. https://doi.org/10.1093/bjps/axv010.

Dawid, R., & McCoy, C. (2023, December). Testability and Viability: Is Inflationary Cosmology "Scientific"? *European Journal for Philosophy of Science*, *13*(4), 51. https://doi.org/10.1007/s13194-023-00556-3.

De Baerdemaeker, S. (2021, January). Method-Driven Experiments and the Search for Dark Matter. *Philosophy of Science*, *88*(1), 124–144. https://doi.org/10.1086/710055.

De Baerdemaeker, S., & Boyd, N. M. (2020, January). Jump Ship, Shift Gears, or Just Keep on Chugging: Assessing the Responses to Tensions between Theory and Evidence in Contemporary Cosmology. *Studies in History and Philosophy of Science Part B: Studies in History and Philosophy of Modern Physics*, *72*, 205–216. https://doi.org/10.1016/j.shpsb.2020.08.002.

De Baerdemaeker, S., & Dawid, R. (2022, August). MOND and Meta-Empirical Theory Assessment. *Synthese, 200*(5), 344. https://doi.org/10.1007/s11229-022-03830-8.

De Baerdemaeker, S., & Schneider, M. D. (2022, March). Better Appreciating the Scale of It: Lemaître and de Sitter at the BAAS Centenary. *HOPOS: The Journal of the International Society for the History of Philosophy of Science, 12*(1), 170–188. https://doi.org/10.1086/719017.

Dellsén, F. (2019, August). Should Scientific Realists Embrace Theoretical Conservatism? *Studies in History and Philosophy of Science Part A, 76*, 30–38. https://doi.org/10.1016/j.shpsa.2018.09.005.

de Swart, J. (2020). Closing in on the Cosmos: Cosmology's Rebirth and the Rise of the Dark Matter Problem. In A. S. Blum, R. Lalli, & J. Renn (Eds.), *The Renaissance of General Relativity in Context* (Vol. 16, pp. 257–284). Cham: Springer International. (Series Title: Einstein Studies) https://doi.org/10.1007/978-3-030-50754-1_8.

de Swart, J. (2022). *How Dark Matter Came to Matter: A History of Missing Mass, 1930-1974* (Doctoral dissertation, University of Amsterdam, Amsterdam). Retrieved 2024-02-26, from https://hdl.handle.net/11245.1/38ae4a9f-a5f9-4d5a-bae3-2a033f567223.

de Swart, J., Bertone, G., & van Dongen, J. (2017, March). How Dark Matter Came to Matter. *Nature Astronomy, 1*(3), 0059. https://doi.org/10.1038/s41550-017-0059.

de Swart, J., Thresher, A. C., & Argüelles, C. A. (2024, June). The Humanities Can Help Make Physics Greener. *Nature Reviews Physics, 6*(7), 404–405. https://doi.org/10.1038/s42254-024-00734-z.

Doboszewski, J., & Elder, J. (2025, March). How Theory-Laden are Observations of Black Holes? *Philosophy of Science*, 1–23. https://doi.org/10.1017/psa.2025.13.

Doboszewski, J., & Lehmkuhl, D. (2023). On the Epistemology of Observational Black Hole Astrophysics. In N. Mills Boyd, S. De Baerdemaeker, K. Heng, & V. Matarese (Eds.), *Philosophy of Astrophysics* (Vol. 472, pp. 225–247). Cham: Springer International. (Series Title: Synthese Library) https://doi.org/10.1007/978-3-031-26618-8_13.

Dougherty, J., & Callender, C. (2016, October). *Black Hole Thermodynamics: More Than an Analogy?* https://philsci-archive.pitt.edu/13195/.

Earman, J. (1995). *Bangs, Crunches, Whimpers, and Shrieks: Singularities and Acausalities in Relativistic Spacetimes*. New York: Oxford University Press.

Earman, J. (2001, January). Lambda: The Constant That Refuses to Die. *Archive for History of Exact Sciences, 55*(3), 189–220. https://doi.org/10.1007/s004070000025.

Earman, J., & Mosterin, J. (1999). A Critical Look at Inflationary Cosmology. *Philosophy of Science*, *66*(1), 1–49.

Eckart, A., Hüttemann, A., Kiefer, C., et al. (2017, May). The Milky Way's Supermassive Black Hole: How Good a Case Is It? A Challenge for Astrophysics & Philosophy of Science. *Foundations of Physics*, *47*(5), 553–624. https://doi.org/10.1007/s10701-017-0079-2.

Eddington, A. (1938). Forty Years of Astronomy. In Needham, J. & W. Pagel (Eds.), *Background to Modern Science* (pp. 115–142). Cambridge: Cambridge University Press.

Einasto, J., Kaasik, A., & Saar, E. (1974, July). Dynamic Evidence on Massive Coronas of Galaxies. *Nature*, *250*(5464), 309–310. https://doi.org/10.1038/250309a0.

Einstein, A. (1917, January). Kosmologische Betrachtungen zur allgemeinen Relativitätstheorie. *Sitzungsberichte der Königlich Preussischen Akademie der Wissenschaften*, 142–152. (ADS Bibcode: 1917SPAW.......142E).

Einstein, A., & de Sitter, W. (1932, March). On the Relation between the Expansion and the Mean Density of the Universe. *Proceedings of the National Academy of Sciences*, *18*(3), 213–214. https://doi.org/10.1073/pnas.18.3.213.

Eisenstein, D. J., Zehavi, I., Hogg, D. W., et al. (2005, December). Detection of the Baryon Acoustic Peak in the Large-Scale Correlation Function of SDSS Luminous Red Galaxies. *The Astrophysical Journal*, *633*(2), 560–574. https://doi.org/10.1086/466512.

Elder, J. (2020). *The Epistemology of Gravitational Wave Astrophysics* (Doctoral Dissertation, University of Notre Dame). https://doi.org/10.7274/3f462517k8t.

Elder, J. (2023a). Black Hole Coalescence: Observation and Model Validation. In L. Patton & E. Curiel (Eds.), *Working toward Solutions in Fluid Dynamics and Astrophysics* (pp. 79–104). Cham: Springer International. (Series Title: SpringerBriefs in History of Science and Technology) https://doi.org/10.1007/978-3-031-25686-8_5.

Elder, J. (2023b). Theory Testing in Gravitational-Wave Astrophysics. In N. Mills Boyd, S. De Baerdemaeker, K. Heng, & V. Matarese (Eds.), *Philosophy of Astrophysics* (Vol. 472, pp. 57–79). Cham: Springer International. (Series Title: Synthese Library) https://doi.org/10.1007/978-3-031-26618-8_4.

Elder, J. (2024, April). Independent Evidence in Multi-messenger Astrophysics. *Studies in History and Philosophy of Science*, *104*, 119–129. https://doi.org/10.1016/j.shpsa.2024.02.006.

Elder, J. (2025, April). On the "Direct Detection" of Gravitational Waves. *Studies in History and Philosophy of Science*, *110*, 1–12. https://doi.org/10.1016/j.shpsa.2025.01.002.

Enander, J., & Thresher, A. C. (2024). *The Colonial Side of Astronomy and What To Do about It with Ann Thresher.* https://poddtoppen.se/podcast/1733859069/spacetime-fika/2-the-colonial-side-of-astronomy-and-what-to-do-about-it-with-ann-thresher (Issued: 2024-04-24).

Evans, P. W., & Thébault, K. P. Y. (2020, August). On the Limits of Experimental Knowledge. *Philosophical Transactions of the Royal Society A: Mathematical, Physical and Engineering Sciences*, *378*(2177), 20190235. https://doi.org/10.1098/rsta.2019.0235.

Event Horizon Telescope. (2022, May). *Astronomers Reveal First Image of the Black Hole at the Heart of Our Galaxy (press release)*. Retrieved 2024-01-29, from https://eventhorizontelescope.org/blog/astronomers-reveal-first-image-black-hole-heart-our-galaxy.

Famaey, B., & McGaugh, S. S. (2012, December). Modified Newtonian Dynamics (MOND): Observational Phenomenology and Relativistic Extensions. *Living Reviews in Relativity*, *15*(1), 10. https://doi.org/10.12942/lrr-2012-10.

Ferreira, P. G., Wolf, W. J., & Read, J. (2025). *The Spectre of Underdetermination in Modern Cosmology.* arXiv. (Version Number: 1) https://doi.org/10.48550/ARXIV.2501.06095.

Field, G. (2021a). The Latest Frontier in Analogue Gravity: New Roles for Analogue Experiments. *PhilSci Archive*. https://philsci-archive.pitt.edu/20365/.

Field, G. (2021b, November). Putting Theory in its Place: The Relationship between Universality Arguments and Empirical Constraints. *The British Journal for the Philosophy of Science*, 718276. https://doi.org/10.1086/718276.

Foundational Aspects of Dark Energy (FADE) Collaboration, Bernardo, H., Bose, B., et al. (2023, January). Modified Gravity Approaches to the Cosmological Constant Problem. *Universe*, *9*(2), 63. https://doi.org/10.3390/universe9020063.

Fox, C., Gueguen, M., Koberinski, A., & Smeenk, C. (2019, August). Philosophy of Cosmology. In *Philosophy*. Oxford University Press. https://doi.org/10.1093/obo/9780195396577-0233.

Freedman, W. L., Madore, B. F., Gibson, B. K., et al. (2001, May). Final Results from the *Hubble Space Telescope Key Project to Measure the Hubble Constant*. *The Astrophysical Journal*, *553*(1), 47–72. https://doi.org/10.1086/320638.

Friedman, A. (1999). Republication of: On the Curvature of Space. *General Relativity and Gravitation*, *31*(12), 1991–2000. (original date: 1922) https://doi.org/10.1023/A:1026751225741.

Galison, P., Doboszewski, J., Elder, J., et al. (2023, February). The Next Generation Event Horizon Telescope Collaboration: History, Philosophy, and Culture. *Galaxies*, *11*(1), 32. doi: https://doi.org/10.3390/galaxies11010032.

Gallagher, S. C., & Smeenk, C. (2023). What's in a Survey? Simulation-Induced Selection Effects in Astronomy. In N. Mills Boyd, S. De Baerdemaeker, K. Heng, & V. Matarese (Eds.), *Philosophy of Astrophysics* (Vol. 472, pp. 207–222). Cham: Springer International. (Series Title: Synthese Library) https://doi.org/10.1007/978-3-031-26618-8_12.

Geha, M., Wechsler, R. H., Mao, Y.-Y., et al. (2017, September). The SAGA Survey. I. Satellite Galaxy Populations around Eight Milky Way Analogs. *The Astrophysical Journal*, *847*(1), 4. https://doi.org/10.3847/1538-4357/aa8626.

Genzel, R., Eckart, A., Ott, T., & Eisenhauer, F. (1997, October). On the Nature of the Dark Mass in the Centre of the Milky Way. *Monthly Notices of the Royal Astronomical Society*, *291*(1), 219–234. https://doi.org/10.1093/mnras/291.1.219.

Ghez, A. M., Klein, B. L., Morris, M., & Becklin, E. E. (1998, December). High Proper-Motion Stars in the Vicinity of Sagittarius A*: Evidence for a Supermassive Black Hole at the Center of Our Galaxy. *The Astrophysical Journal*, *509*(2), 678–686. https://doi.org/10.1086/306528.

Ghez, A. M., Morris, M., Becklin, E. E., Tanner, A., & Kremenek, T. (2000, September). The Accelerations of Stars Orbiting the Milky Way's Central Black Hole. *Nature*, *407*(6802), 349–351. https://doi.org/10.1038/35030032.

Godard Palluet, A., & Gueguen, M. (2024, January). Navigating in the Dark. *Philosophy of Science*, 91(5), 1316–1326. https://doi.org/10.1017/psa.2023.175.

Gueguen, M. (n.d.). *A Tension within Code Comparisons*.

Gueguen, M. (2020, December). On Robustness in Cosmological Simulations. *Philosophy of Science*, *87*(5), 1197–1208. https://doi.org/10.1086/710839.

Gueguen, M. (2023). A Crack in the Track of the Hubble Constant. In N. Mills Boyd, S. De Baerdemaeker, K. Heng, & V. Matarese (Eds.), *Philosophy of Astrophysics* (Vol. 472, pp. 33–55). Cham: Springer International. (Series Title: Synthese Library) https://doi.org/10.1007/978-3-031-26618-8_3.

Guralp, G. (2020, May). The Evidence for the Accelerating Universe: Endorsement and Robust Consistency. *European Journal for Philosophy of Science*, *10*(2), 21. https://doi.org/10.1007/s13194-020-0276-2.

Guth, A. H. (1981, January). Inflationary Universe: A Possible Solution to the Horizon and Flatness Problems. *Physical Review D*, *23*(2), 347–356. https://doi.org/10.1103/PhysRevD.23.347.

Guth, A. H. (2007, June). Eternal Inflation and its Implications. *Journal of Physics A: Mathematical and Theoretical*, *40*(25), 6811–6826. https://doi.org/10.1088/1751-8113/40/25/S25.

Guth, A. H., Kaiser, D. I., Linde, A. D., et al. (2017). A Cosmic Controversy. *Scientific American*, *317*(1), 5–7.

Guth, A. H., Kaiser, D. I., & Nomura, Y. (2014, June). Inflationary Paradigm after Planck 2013. *Physics Letters B*, *733*, 112–119. https://doi.org/10.1016/j.physletb.2014.03.020.

Guth, A. H., & Pi, S.-Y. (1982, October). Fluctuations in the New Inflationary Universe. *Physical Review Letters*, *49*(15), 1110–1113. https://doi.org/10.1103/PhysRevLett.49.1110.

Hacking, I. (1983). *Representing and Intervening: Introductory Topics in the Philosophy of Natural Science* (1st ed.). New York: Cambridge University Press. https://doi.org/10.1017/CBO9780511814563.

Hacking, I. (1988). Philosophers of Experiment. *PSA: Proceedings of the Biennial Meeting of the Philosophy of Science Association*, *1988*(2), 147–156. https://doi.org/10.1086/psaprocbienmeetp.1988.2.192879.

Hacking, I. (1989). Extragalactic Reality: The Case of Gravitational Lensing. *Philosophy of Science*, *56*(4), 555–581.

Hawking, S. W. (1975, August). Particle Creation by Black Holes. *Communications in Mathematical Physics*, *43*(3), 199–220. https://doi.org/10.1007/BF02345020.

Holmes, A. L. (2024). *Climbing the Cosmic Distance Ladder* (Doctoral dissertation, Notre Dame). https://curate.nd.edu/articles/dataset/Climbing_the_Cosmic_Distance_Ladder/26103637.

Hubble, E. (1929, March). A Relation between Distance and Radial Velocity among Extra-Galactic Nebulae. *Proceedings of the National Academy of Science*, *15*, 168–173. https://doi.org/10.1073/pnas.15.3.168.

Hubble, E., & Humason, M. L. (1931, July). The Velocity-Distance Relation among Extra-Galactic Nebulae. *The Astrophysical Journal*, *74*, 43. (ADS Bibcode: 1931ApJ....74...43H) https://doi.org/10.1086/143323.

Ijjas, A., Steinhardt, P. J., & Loeb, A. (2014, September). Inflationary Schism. *Physics Letters B*, *736*, 142–146. https://doi.org/10.1016/j.physletb.2014.07.012

Ijjas, A., Steinhardt, P. J., & Loeb, A. (2017, January). Pop Goes the Universe. *Scientific American*, *316*(2), 32–39. https://doi.org/10.1038/scientificamerican0217-32.

Jacquart, M. (2020, December). Observations, Simulations, and Reasoning in Astrophysics. *Philosophy of Science*, *87*(5), 1209–1220. https://doi.org/10.1086/710544.

Jacquart, M. (2021, October). ΛCDM and MOND: A Debate about Models or Theory? *Studies in History and Philosophy of Science Part A*, *89*, 226–234. https://doi.org/10.1016/j.shpsa.2021.07.001.

Kadowaki, K. (2023). Simulation Verification in Practice. In N. Mills Boyd, S. De Baerdemaeker, K. Heng, & V. Matarese (Eds.), *Philosophy of Astrophysics* (Vol. 472, pp. 151–170). Cham: Springer International. (Series Title: Synthese Library) https://doi.org/10.1007/978-3-031-26618-8_9.

Kahanamoku, S., Alegado, R. A., Kagawa-Viviani, A., et al. (2020). *A Native Hawaiian-Led Summary of the Current Impact of Constructing the Thirty Meter Telescope on Maunakea*. arXiv. (arXiv:2001.00970 [astro-ph, physics:physics]) https://doi.org/10.6084/m9.figshare.c.4805619.

Koberinski, A. (2021, August). Problems with the Cosmological Constant Problem. In C. Wüthrich, B. Le Bihan, and N. Huggett (eds.), *Philosophy beyond Spacetime* (pp. 260–280). Oxford: Oxford University Press. https://doi.org/10.1093/oso/9780198844143.003.0012.

Koberinski, A., Falck, B., & Smeenk, C. (2023, March). Contemporary Philosophical Perspectives on the Cosmological Constant. *Universe*, *9*(3), 134. https://doi.org/10.3390/universe9030134.

Koberinski, A., & Smeenk, C. (2023, April). Λ and the Limits of Effective Field Theory. *Philosophy of Science*, *90*(2), 454–474. https://doi.org/10.1017/psa.2022.16.

Kolb, E. W., & Turner, M. (1990). *The Early Universe* (No. 69). Oxford: Westview Press.

Kosso, P. (2013, May). Evidence of Dark Matter, and the Interpretive Role of General Relativity. *Studies in History and Philosophy of Science Part B: Studies in History and Philosophy of Modern Physics*, *44*(2), 143–147. https://doi.org/10.1016/j.shpsb.2012.11.005.

Lemaître, G. (1927, January). Un Univers Homogène de Masse Constante et de Rayon Croissant Rendant Compte de la Vitesse Radiale des Nébuleuses Extra-Galactiques. *Annales de la Société Scientifique de Bruxelles*, *47*, 49–59. (ADS Bibcode: 1927ASSB...47...49L).

Licquia, T. C., Newman, J. A., & Bershady, M. A. (2016, December). Does the Milky Way Obey Spiral Galaxy Scaling Relations? *The Astrophysical Journal*, *833*(2), 220. https://doi.org/10.3847/1538-4357/833/2/220.

Long, W. R. (1994, April). Dispute Threatens Observatory Project in Chile: Astronomy: Legal Wrangling Imperils Plan for the World's Most Powerful

Telescope in the Atacama Desert. *Los Angeles Times*. Retrieved 2024-04-30, www.latimes.com/archives/la-xpm-1994-08-06-mn-24135-story.html.

Manchak, J. B. (2011, July). What Is a Physically Reasonable Space-Time? *Philosophy of Science*, *78*(3), 410–420. https://doi.org/10.1086/660301.

Mao, Y.-Y., Geha, M.,Wechsler, R. H., et al. (2021, February). The SAGA Survey. II. Building a Statistical Sample of Satellite Systems around Milky Way–like Galaxies. *The Astrophysical Journal*, *907*(2), 85. https://doi.org/10.3847/1538-4357/abce58.

Martens, N. (2022, February). Dark Matter Realism. *Foundations of Physics*, *52*(1), 16. https://doi.org/10.1007/s10701-021-00524-y.

Martens, N., Carretero Sahuquillo, M., Scholz, E., Lehmkuhl, D., & Krämer, M. (2022, February). Integrating Dark Matter, Modified Gravity, and the Humanities. *Studies in History and Philosophy of Science*, *91*, A1–A5. https://doi.org/10.1016/j.shpsa.2021.08.015.

Martens, N., & Lehmkuhl, D. (2020a, November). Cartography of the Space of Theories: An Interpretational Chart for Fields that are Both (Dark) Matter and Spacetime. *Studies in History and Philosophy of Science Part B: Studies in History and Philosophy of Modern Physics*, *72*, 217–236. https://doi.org/10.1016/j.shpsb.2020.08.004.

Martens, N., & Lehmkuhl, D. (2020b, November). Dark Matter = Modified Gravity? Scrutinising the Spacetime–Matter Distinction through the Modified Gravity/ Dark Matter Lens. *Studies in History and Philosophy of Science Part B: Studies in History and Philosophy of Modern Physics*, *72*, 237–250. https://doi.org/10.1016/j.shpsb.2020.08.003.

Martin, J., & Brandenberger, R. (2001, May). The Trans-Planckian Problem of Inflationary Cosmology. *Physical Review D*, *63*(12), 123501. https://doi.org/10.1103/PhysRevD.63.123501.

Massimi, M. (2018, January). Three Problems about Multi-Scale Modelling in Cosmology. *Studies in History and Philosophy of Science Part B: Studies in History and Philosophy of Modern Physics*, *64*, 26–38. https://doi.org/10.1016/j.shpsb.2018.04.002.

Matarese, V., & McCoy, C. (2024, October). When "Replicability" Is More than Just "Reliability": The Hubble Constant Controversy. *Studies in History and Philosophy of Science*, *107*, 1–10. https://doi.org/10.1016/j.shpsa.2024.07.005.

Mathie, A. (2023). Black Holes and Analogy. In N. Mills Boyd, S. De Baerdemaeker, K. Heng, & V. Matarese (Eds.), *Philosophy of Astrophysics* (Vol. 472, pp. 249–276). Cham: Springer International. (Series Title: Synthese Library) https://doi.org/10.1007/978-3-031-26618-8_14.

McCoy, C. (2015, August). Does Inflation Solve the Hot Big Bang Model's Fine-Tuning Problems? *Studies in History and Philosophy of Science Part B: Studies in History and Philosophy of Modern Physics*, *51*, 23–36. https://doi.org/10.1016/j.shpsb.2015.06.002.

McCoy, C. (2017, December). Can Typicality Arguments Dissolve Cosmology's Flatness Problem? *Philosophy of Science*, *84*(5), 1239–1252. https://doi.org/10.1086/694109.

McCoy, C. (2019, December). Epistemic Justification and Methodological Luck in Inflationary Cosmology. *The British Journal for the Philosophy of Science*, *70*(4), 1003–1028. https://doi.org/10.1093/bjps/axy014.

McGaugh, S. S. (2015, February). A Tale of Two Paradigms: The Mutual Incommensurability of ΛCDM and MOND. *Canadian Journal of Physics*, *93*(2), 250–259. https://doi.org/10.1139/cjp-2014-0203.

Merritt, D. (2017, February). Cosmology and Convention. *Studies in History and Philosophy of Science Part B: Studies in History and Philosophy of Modern Physics*, *57*, 41–52. https://doi.org/10.1016/j.shpsb.2016.12.002.

Merritt, D. (2020). *A Philosophical Approach to MOND: Assessing the Milgromian Research Program in Cosmology* (1st ed.). Cambridge University Press. https://doi.org/10.1017/9781108610926.

Merritt, D. (2021, December). Feyerabend's Rule and Dark Matter. *Synthese*, *199*(3-4), 8921–8942. https://doi.org/10.1007/s11229-021-03188-3.

Meskhidze, H. (2023). (What) Do We Learn from Code Comparisons? A Case Study of Self-Interacting Dark Matter Implementations. In N. Mills Boyd, S. De Baerdemaeker, K. Heng, & V. Matarese (Eds.), *Philosophy of Astrophysics* (Vol. 472, pp. 171–186). Cham: Springer International. (Series Title: Synthese Library) https://doi.org/10.1007/978-3-031-26618-8_10.

Milgrom, M. (1983a, July). A Modification of the Newtonian Dynamics as a Possible Alternative to the Hidden Mass Hypothesis. *The Astrophysical Journal*, *270*, 365. https://doi.org/10.1086/161130.

Milgrom, M. (1983b, July). A Modification of the Newtonian Dynamics - Implications for Galaxies. *The Astrophysical Journal*, *270*, 371. https://doi.org/10.1086/161131.

Milgrom, M. (1983c, July). A Modification of the Newtonian Dynamics - Implications for Galaxy Systems. *The Astrophysical Journal*, *270*, 384. https://doi.org/10.1086/161132.

Milgrom, M. (2020, August). MOND vs. Dark Matter in Light of Historical Parallels. *Studies in History and Philosophy of Science Part B: Studies in History and Philosophy of Modern Physics*, *71*, 170–195. https://doi.org/10.1016/j.shpsb.2020.02.004.

Norton, J. D. (2021, July). Eternal Inflation: When Probabilities Fail. *Synthese*, *198*(S16), 3853–3875. https://doi.org/10.1007/s11229-018-1734-7.

Novick, A., Currie, A. M., McQueen, E. W., & Brouwer, N. L. (2020, April). Kon-Tiki Experiments. *Philosophy of Science*, *87*(2), 213–236. https://doi.org/10.1086/707553.

NSF. (2017). *Environmental Impact Statement for the Arecibo Observatory Arecibo, Puerto Rico Final* (Tech. Rep.). www.nsf.gov/mps/ast/env_impact_reviews/arecibo/arecibo_feis.jsp.

O'Raifeartaigh, C., McCann, B., Nahm, W., & Mitton, S. (2014, September). Einstein's Steady-State Theory: An Abandoned Model of the Cosmos. *European Physical Journal H*, *39*, 353–367. (ADS Bibcode: 2014EPJH...39..353O) https://doi.org/10.1140/epjh/e2014-50011-x.

Ostriker, J. P., Peebles, P. J. E., & Yahil, A. (1974, October). The Size and Mass of Galaxies, and the Mass of the Universe. *The Astrophysical Journal*, *193*, L1. https://doi.org/10.1086/181617.

O'Raifeartaigh, C., & Mitton, S. (2018, December). Interrogating the Legend of Einstein's "Biggest Blunder". *Physics in Perspective*, *20*(4), 318–341. https://doi.org/10.1007/s00016-018-0228-9.

Planck Collaboration, Ade, P. A. R., Aghanim, N., Armitage-Caplan, C., et al. (2014, December). Planck 2013 Results. XXIV. Constraints on Primordial Non-Gaussianity. *Astronomy & Astrophysics*, *571*, A24. https://doi.org/10.1051/0004-6361/201321554.

Planck Collaboration, Aghanim, N., Akrami, Y., et al. (2020, September). Planck 2018 Results. VI. Cosmological Parameters. *Astronomy & Astrophysics*, *641*, A6. (arXiv:1807.06209 [astro-ph]) https://doi.org/10.1051/0004-6361/201833910.

Planck Collaboration, Akrami, Y., Arroja, F., et al. (2020, September). Planck 2018 Results: X. Constraints on Inflation. *Astronomy & Astrophysics*, *641*, A10. https://doi.org/10.1051/0004-6361/201833887.

Prescod-Weinstein, C. (2021). *The Disordered Cosmos: A Journey into Dark Matter, Spacetime, and Dreams Deferred* (1st ed.). New York: Bold Type Books.

Prescod-Weinstein, C., Walkowicz, L. M., Tuttle, S., et al. (2020, January). *Reframing Astronomical Research through an Anticolonial Lens – for TMT and beyond.* arXiv. (arXiv:2001.00674 [astro-ph]).

Psillos, S. (1999). *Scientific Realism: How Science Tracks Truth* (??th ed.). London: Routledge. https://doi.org/10.4324/9780203979648.

Rubin, V. C., & Ford, W. K., Jr. (1970, February). Rotation of the Andromeda Nebula from a Spectroscopic Survey of Emission Regions. *The Astrophysical Journal*, *159*, 379. https://doi.org/10.1086/150317.

Sandage, A. (1958, May). Current Problems in the Extragalactic Distance Scale. *The Astrophysical Journal, 127*, 513. (ADS Bibcode: 1958ApJ...127..513S) https://doi.org/10.1086/146483.

Sandell, M. (2010). Astronomy and Experimentation. *Techne, 14*(3), 252–269. https://doi.org/10.5840/techne201014325.

Schneider, M. D. (2020, January). What's the Problem with the Cosmological Constant? *Philosophy of Science, 87*(1), 1–20. https://doi.org/10.1086/706076.

Schneider, M. D. (2021, December). Trans-Planckian Philosophy of Cosmology. *Studies in History and Philosophy of Science Part A, 90*, 184–193. https://doi.org/10.1016/j.shpsa.2021.10.001.

Schneider, M. D. (2022, March). Betting on Future Physics. *The British Journal for the Philosophy of Science, 73*(1), 161–183. https://doi.org/10.1093/bjps/axz040.

Schneider, M. D. (2023, August). On Efforts to Decouple Early Universe Cosmology and Quantum Gravity Phenomenology. *Foundations of Physics, 53*(4), 77. https://doi.org/10.1007/s10701-023-00720-y.

Schneider, M. D., & De Baerdemaeker, S. (2023, April). Cosmology and Empire. *Nature Astronomy, 7*(4), 368–370. https://doi.org/10.1038/s41550-023-01940-y.

Shapere, D. (1993, March). Discussion: Astronomy and Antirealism. *Philosophy of Science, 60*(1), 134–150. https://doi.org/10.1086/289722.

Simões, A., & Sousa, A. M. (2019). *Einstein Eddington e o Eclipse: Impressões de Viagem = Einstein Eddington and the Eclipse: Travel Impressions* (1a edição ed.) (No. 8). Lisboa: Chili com Carne.

Skulberg, E., & Elder, J. (forthcoming). What Is a "direct" Image of a Shadow? A History and Epistemology of "Directness" in Black Hole Research. *Centaurus*. (status: forthcoming) doi: https://doi.org/10.1484/J.CNT.5.144759.

Smeenk, C. (2014, May). Predictability Crisis in Early Universe Cosmology. *Studies in History and Philosophy of Science Part B: Studies in History and Philosophy of Modern Physics, 46*, 122–133. https://doi.org/10.1016/j.shpsb.2013.11.003.

Smeenk, C. (2017, January). Testing Inflation. In K. Chamcham, J. Silk, J. D. Barrow, & S. Saunders (Eds.), *The Philosophy of Cosmology* (1st ed., pp. 206–227). New York: Cambridge University Press. https://doi.org/10.1017/9781316535783.011.

Smeenk, C. (2019, March). Gaining Access to the Early Universe. In R. Dardashti, R. Dawid, & K. Thébault (Eds.), *Why Trust a Theory?* (1st ed., pp. 315–336). New York: Cambridge University Press. https://doi.org/10.1017/9781108671224.021.

Smeenk, C. (2020, August). Some Reflections on the Structure of Cosmological Knowledge. *Studies in History and Philosophy of Science Part B: Studies in History and Philosophy of Modern Physics*, *71*, 220–231. https://doi.org/10.1016/j.shpsb.2020.05.004.

Smeenk, C., & Ellis, G. (2017). Philosophy of Cosmology. In E. N. Zalta (Ed.), *The Stanford Encyclopedia of Philosophy* (Winter 2017 ed.). Metaphysics Research Lab, Stanford University. https://plato.stanford.edu/archives/win2017/entries/cosmology/.

Smeenk, C., & Gallagher, S. C. (2020, December). Validating the Universe in a Box. *Philosophy of Science*, *87*(5), 1221–1233. https://doi.org/10.1086/710627.

Smeenk, C., & Weatherall, J. O. (2023, October). Dark Energy or Modified Gravity? *Philosophy of Science*, *1–10*. https://doi.org/10.1017/psa.2023.143.

Spergel, D. N., Verde, L., Peiris, H. V., et al. (2003, September). First-Year *Wilkinson Microwave Anisotropy Probe* (*WMAP*) Observations: Determination of Cosmological Parameters. *The Astrophysical Journal Supplement Series*, *148*(1), 175–194. https://doi.org/10.1086/377226.

Sus, A. (2014, February). Dark Matter, the Equivalence Principle and Modified Gravity. *Studies in History and Philosophy of Science Part B: Studies in History and Philosophy of Modern Physics*, *45*, 66–71. https://doi.org/10.1016/j.shpsb.2013.12.005.

Suárez, M. (2023). Stellar Structure Models Revisited: Evidence and Data in Asteroseismology. In N. Mills Boyd, S. De Baerdemaeker, K. Heng, & V. Matarese (Eds.), *Philosophy of Astrophysics* (Vol. 472, pp. 111–129). Cham: Springer International. (Series Title: Synthese Library) https://doi.org/10.1007/978-3-031-26618-8_7.

Swanner, L. (2013). *Mountains of Controversy: Narrative and the Making of Contested Landscapes in Postwar American Astronomy* (Doctoral dissertation, Harvard University). http://nrs.harvard.edu/urn-3:HUL.InstRepos:11156816.

Swanner, L. (2017, June). Instruments of Science or Conquest? Neocolonialism and Modern American Astronomy. *Historical Studies in the Natural Sciences*, *47*(3), 293–319. https://doi.org/10.1525/hsns.2017.47.3.293.

Thébault, K. (2019, March). What Can We Learn from Analogue Experiments? In R. Dardashti, R. Dawid, & K. Thébault (Eds.), *Why Trust a Theory?* (1st ed., pp. 184–201). New York: Cambridge University Press. https://doi.org/10.1017/9781108671224.014.

Unruh, W. G. (1981, May). Experimental Black-Hole Evaporation? *Physical Review Letters*, *46*(21), 1351–1353. https://doi.org/10.1103/PhysRevLett.46.1351.

Vanderburgh, W. L. (2003, October). The Dark Matter Double Bind: Astrophysical Aspects of the Evidential Warrant for General Relativity. *Philosophy of Science, 70*(4), 812–832. https://doi.org/10.1086/378866.

Vanderburgh, W. L. (2005, December). The Methodological Value of Coincidences: Further Remarks on Dark Matter and the Astrophysical Warrant for General Relativity. *Philosophy of Science, 72*(5), 1324–1335. https://doi.org/10.1086/508971.

Vanderburgh, W. L. (2014, August). On the Interpretive Role of Theories of Gravity and 'Ugly' Solutions to the Total Evidence for Dark Matter. *Studies in History and Philosophy of Science Part B: Studies in History and Philosophy of Modern Physics, 47*, 62–67. https://doi.org/10.1016/j.shpsb.2014.05.008.

Vaynberg, E. (2024, August). Realism and the Detection of Dark Matter. *Synthese, 204*(3), 82. https://doi.org/10.1007/s11229-024-04728-3.

Wallace, D. (2018, January). The Case for Black Hole Thermodynamics Part I: Phenomenological Thermodynamics. *Studies in History and Philosophy of Science Part B: Studies in History and Philosophy of Modern Physics, 64*, 52–67. https://doi.org/10.1016/j.shpsb.2018.05.002.

Wallace, D. (2019, May). The Case for Black Hole Thermodynamics Part II: Statistical Mechanics. *Studies in History and Philosophy of Science Part B: Studies in History and Philosophy of Modern Physics, 66*, 103–117. https://doi.org/10.1016/j.shpsb.2018.10.006.

Wallace, D. (2021, December). *Quantum Gravity at Low Energies.* arXiv. (arXiv:2112.12235 [gr-qc]).

Weatherall, J. O. (2021, March). *The Philosophy behind Dark Matter.* University of Pittsburgh: Centre for Philosophy of Science. Retrieved 2024-04-12, from www.youtube.com/watch?v=0QSa45ZPbHg.

Weinberg, S. (1972). *Gravitation and Cosmology: Principles and Applications of the General Theory of Relativity.* New York: Wiley.

Weinberg, S. (1989, January). The Cosmological Constant Problem. *Reviews of Modern Physics, 61*(1), 1–23. https://doi.org/10.1103/RevModPhys.61.1.

Weisberg, M., Jacquart, M., Madore, B., & Seidel, M. (2018, December). The Dark Galaxy Hypothesis. *Philosophy of Science, 85*(5), 1204–1215. https://doi.org/10.1086/699694.

Wolf, W. J. (2024, February). Cosmological Inflation and Meta-empirical Theory Assessment. *Studies in History and Philosophy of Science, 103*, 146–158. https://doi.org/10.1016/j.shpsa.2023.12.006.

Wolf, W. J., & Ferreira, P. G. (2023, November). Underdetermination of Dark Energy. *Physical Review D, 108*(10), 103519. https://doi.org/10.1103/PhysRevD.108.103519.

Wolf, W. J., & Thébault, K. P. Y. (2023, March). Explanatory Depth in Primordial Cosmology: A Comparative Study of Inflationary and Bouncing Paradigms. *The British Journal for the Philosophy of Science*, 725096. https://doi.org/10.1086/725096.

Workman, R. L., Burkert, V. D., Crede, V., et al. (2022, August). Review of Particle Physics. *Progress of Theoretical and Experimental Physics, 2022*(8), 083C01. https://doi.org/10.1093/ptep/ptac097.

Yao, S. (2023, December). Excavation in the Sky: Historical Inference in Astronomy. *Philosophy of Science, 90*(5), 1385–1395. https://doi.org/10.1017/psa.2023.22.

Yetman, C. C. (2023). Annotated Bibliography. In N. Mills Boyd, S. De Baerdemaeker, K. Heng, & V. Matarese (Eds.), *Philosophy of Astrophysics* (Vol. 472, pp. 305–332). Cham: Springer International. (Series Title: Synthese Library) https://doi.org/10.1007/978-3-031-26618-8_17.

Zwicky, F. (2009, January). Republication of: The Redshift of Extragalactic Nebulae. *General Relativity and Gravitation, 41*(1), 207–224. (original date: 1933) https://doi.org/10.1007/s10714-008-0707-4.

Acknowledgments

I am indebted to Nora Mills Boyd, Richard Dawid, Guilherme Franzmann, James Nguyen, Mike D. Schneider, and two anonymous referees for extensive discussions and comments on earlier drafts. I am also grateful to James Owen Weatherall for the opportunity to write this Element, and for the patience along the way. This work was supported by a grant from Riksbankens Jubileumsfond (grant no. P22-0511).

Cambridge Elements

The Philosophy of Physics

James Owen Weatherall
University of California, Irvine

James Owen Weatherall is Chancellor's Professor in the Department of Logic and Philosophy of Science at the University of California, Irvine. He is the author, with Cailin O'Connor, of The Misinformation Age: How False Beliefs Spread (Yale, 2019), which was selected as a New York Times Editors' Choice and Recommended Reading by Scientific American. His previous books were Void: The Strange Physics of Nothing (Yale, 2016) and the New York Times bestseller The Physics of Wall Street: A Brief History of Predicting the Unpredictable (Houghton Mifflin Harcourt, 2013). He has published approximately 50 peer-reviewed research articles in journals in leading physics and philosophy of science journals and has delivered over 100 invited academic talks and public lectures.

About the Series

This Cambridge Elements series provides concise and structured introductions to all the central topics in the philosophy of physics. The Elements in the series are written by distinguished senior scholars and bright junior scholars with relevant expertise, producing balanced, comprehensive coverage of multiple perspectives in the philosophy of physics.

Cambridge Elements

The Philosophy of Physics

Elements in the Series

The Temporal Asymmetry of Causation
Alison Fernandes

Special Relativity
James Read

Philosophy of Particle Physics
Porter Williams

Foundations of Statistical Mechanics
Roman Frigg and Charlotte Werndl

From Randomness and Entropy to the Arrow of Time
Lena Zuchowski

Philosophy of Physical Magnitudes
Niels C. M. Martens

The Philosophy of Symmetry
Nicholas Joshua Yii Wye Teh

Laws of Physics
Eddy Keming Chen

Foundations of General Relativity
Samuel C. Fletcher

Gauge Theory and the Geometrization of Physics
Henrique De Andrade Gomes

Causation in Physics
Christopher Gregory Weaver

Philosophy of Cosmology and Astrophysics
Siska De Baerdemaeker

A full series listing is available at: www.cambridge.org/EPPH

For EU product safety concerns, contact us at Calle de José Abascal, 56–1°,
28003 Madrid, Spain or eugpsr@cambridge.org.

www.ingramcontent.com/pod-product-compliance
Lightning Source LLC
LaVergne TN
LVHW011852060526
838200LV00054B/4297